LESSONS FROM THE GOLF GURU

WIT, WISDOM, MIND-TRICKS, & MYSTICISM

FOR GOLF AND LIFE

Mike E. Dowd, PGA

TABLE OF CONTENTS

PREFACE

*"Alexander, Caesar, Charlemagne, and myself
founded empires; but upon what foundation did we
rest the creations of our genius? Upon force. Jesus
Christ founded an empire upon love; and at this
hour millions of men would die for him."*
– Napoleon Bonaparte

Before we begin, I think it's important to briefly explain
the logic behind the foundation and layout of this book as well as
exactly what it is and what it isn't. First, what it's not... This isn't
a book about Hinduism, Buddhism, Sikhism, Catholicism, or any
other religious *ism* typically associated with Gurus. Sure, there
are some for whom the sport of golf almost qualifies as a religion,
and there are quotes, lessons, and wisdom herein that has been

passed on by some of history's more famous Gurus, but as *The Golf Guru,* my title is a bit more metaphorical in nature, and whatever wisdom I possess comes as much from experience as it does from the ancients.

Guru is a Sanskrit term for teacher or master. In the Hindu Guru Tradition, it describes the experiential wisdom that is transmitted from teacher to student, which, on the surface, sounds pretty darn close to how I find myself spending a great many hours at the golf course each day. For Buddhists, Buddha is the ultimate Guru, and he supposedly taught that the path to enlightenment was through "The Middle Way," which does ironically sound a lot like the path (or region of the fairway) most of us golfers are seeking on our own journeys to enlightenment. At the same time, that just sounds a little too curiously similar to me as the "Everything in Moderation" mantra my Italian father-in-law is so fond of trotting out after his second or third glass of wine. Wise words for sure, but far from enlightening or anything that would remotely compel me to suggest to that God-fearing Catholic that he might actually be a closet Buddhist. And, as I said, since this isn't really a book about Buddhism, I've made sure to leave out pretty much anything that would actually require you to be a practicing Shabhala Warrior in order to understand.

This also (hopefully) isn't just another one of those wistful and wishful attempts to draw the comparisons between golf and life wrapped in a little rehashed wisdom, corny mysticism, and a handful of ancient quotes. O.K., well, as I said before, there's a little of that stuff in here. I love the timeless wisdom of famous quotes, and golf really can at times be a metaphor for life, but at least this isn't a dry clinical text that forgoes any attempts at entertainment in favor of more serious educational discussions because, hey, I want you to learn something, but I also want you to stick around long enough to get to the last few chapters (some of the best in my beta-readers' opinions) and maybe even want to read my next book.

This also isn't a traditional nuts 'n' bolts golf instruction manual. Sure, I'm a golf professional, and while I'm fairly adept at fixing hooks and slices, I get enough talk of tucking your right elbow, keeping your left arm straight, keeping your head down, the merits of the Stack 'N' Tilt vs. the A Position vs. the 2-Plane Swing, and all of the other stereotypical swing mechanic discussion topics in my day job. And besides, I said this wasn't a dry clinical text and I've yet to read any attempts to discuss swing mechanics that were interesting enough without at least pictures or video that you wouldn't be nodding off before chapter two.

So what exactly is this…? Well, if you get past the introduction (and the sarcasm), this is a golf book, primarily, but possibly just a bit more if you're really paying attention. I did mention I'm a golf professional, right? So what else would you expect me to write about? Speaking of the introduction, however, that brief segment is where I will relate the story of how, as a small-town club professional working in the Cowboy Capital of the World, I ultimately became *The Golf Guru* and was subsequently compelled to write this book. And while its form and content are completely dissimilar from the rest of the book, I felt it a story worth telling and, because this is my book, I can do that. If you just can't wait to get to the meat and potatoes, however, you can skip it, but give it a moment. Ultimately I think you'll understand why it serves a purpose in and of itself, while simultaneously lending a bit of a backdrop.

As far as those meat and potatoes go, while this may not be the most traditional meal you could be served up if you're hungry for a better golf game, I promise it still qualifies as edible, and by the fact that you're reading this, I'll assume your tastes trend towards the exotic. Much of the material should help you with what is commonly referred to as "the mental side of the game," but it's really a veritable smorgasbord: a collection of lessons, reflections, and musings on the game, the state of the game, and the characters who play it, along with a healthy dose of the latest scientific research, clever anecdotes, random stories, ancient mysticism, and timeless wisdom. This goes along with more than a few handfuls of practices that we should all likely adopt to improve both our golf and our lives, while learning to enjoy and appreciate every moment of both more along the way.

So now that I've told you what this book is and what it isn't, I think it's important to mention a little something about the layout to hopefully answer a few likely questions and explain the logic behind it. Much of this book wasn't originally conceived as such but was culled from a loose collection of writings on the game that I had published via my weekly column or blog over a period of a few years and then expanded upon after further reflection. Given that fact, I wanted to organize them in a way that would not only make sense, but would also have a collective flow that serves a greater purpose. With this goal in mind, I've attempted to arrange each lesson or chapter so that it builds upon the foundation laid by the previous, forging a path that will hopefully make each step along the journey just a little bit easier than the last.

The book is broken down into ten sections, each with a collection of lessons and tales centered around three closely related emotions, states of being, and/or qualities of character that each of us possesses or displays (to varying degrees depending upon our individual makeup). We begin the journey focused on some of the more negative qualities or emotions that we all have or must deal with from time to time and work our way through progressively more benign ones, until we find ourselves in the end having navigated to the more positive side of the spectrum. And while common sense may be enough of an explanation for some as to why I chose to deal with the worst things first, I want to assure you there is at least a little more to it than that. Yes, there is actually some science (or pseudoscience) behind the organizational method to my apparent madness and the genius of what I will call my master plan.

The thought behind the layout of this book first occurred to me a few years ago when I was reading something about quantum physics, which laid out a chart that had been developed based upon the findings of related studies. Now, hopefully I can stop some of you in mid-eye roll by stating that I am fully aware that amongst the things being attributed to the findings in quantum physics are everything from the thought-manifesting realities espoused by the hordes of "Law of Attraction" disciples to the "secret to life itself" claims of the rabbit-hole-burrowing quantum mysticists to the sobering cries of an ardent host of realists who hold that most everything being attributed to quantum physics these days is nothing more than a bunch of pseudoscience whose theories have been hijacked by charlatans selling books and other self-help products to the patently gullible. But stick with me for a moment, because in this instance, even if the science that backs it up is still a bit controversial and difficult to comprehend, the premise rings of enough truth that I believe it merits at least a little further exploration and can work easily as a foundation for this book, even if you count yourself among the quantum non-believers.

Now for starters, the nexus of quantum physics is undeniable. Everything is made up of energy: you, me, your seven iron, your poorly trained golf ball, the trees, the grass, your opponent, and even the hole. And the energy that makes up you vibrates at a frequency that can be measured on an oscilloscope. Now forgive me if you've heard this before, but here is where things start to get a bit fuzzy. Apparently the energy you radiate, somewhat like a magnet, attracts other similar energy. With this thought in mind, some have concluded that you will subsequently attract the type of energy (people, circumstances, and situations) that is most similar to what you are giving off. Now taking it one step further, supposedly the frequency of the energy you radiate is directly attributable to your mood and the types of emotions/qualities that you most commonly display. A chart that was developed from these findings lists the most negative emotions and qualities, such as fear and anger, at one end and works its way through progressively until you ultimately arrive at things like appreciation, gratitude, and love at the other.

Now, not being the owner of an oscilloscope and being naturally inclined towards the positive, I have decided to accept this premise on faith because, well, I just like the fact that it purports to give a scientific explanation for something I've always just instinctively known. Positive people attract positive people and, by extension, positive situations and events, for the most part. And as you should have now concluded, negative people do the same (meaning negative people, situations, and events). Now, I know for the naysayers this may sound like an over-simplified and wishful attempt to use science to explain what is just plain common sense. Let's suppose for a moment, however, that there is more to it than that and just maybe there is an actual physical connection between the Eeyore attitude you've been displaying on the course and your struggles to improve, the difficulties you have had in finding a game, or even the unbelievable amount of bad luck you always seem to experience. And so by extension, if you don't first deal with eliminating all that fear, anger, and negativity, it will ultimately be impossible to just wake up one morning and find yourself magically transformed into that ridiculously positive and almost annoyingly popular guy or gal at your club for whom the game and life seems almost easy or charmed or the one who seems to be forever getting those so-called "member" bounces.

Now, as I stated previously, this is first and foremost a golf book, but hopefully I wrote this in a way that makes it apparent how a great deal of the lessons and stories contained herein are not applicable just to golf, but to the game of life as well. It can be read straight through, and while some of the thoughts will hopefully prove to be akin to mentally flipping a light switch, if you do read it cover to cover, you will likely get more out of it if you go back and pick out the particular things you need to work on most and tackle those topics one at a time. Need a process to help you break those old habits or start building some new ones? There's a chapter for that *(Start at the Finish Line)*. So once you're past the introduction, roll up your sleeves and prepare for things to get a bit messy, because, as Ben Hogan used to say, the first secret is in the dirt, as your journey starts with fear and anger. But if things go well, hopefully, when all is said and done, you'll remember why the game and life are so great and, in the end, find yourself in love...

INTRODUCTION

"Even the journey of a thousand miles
begins with a single step."
– Lao Tzu

A long time ago in a galaxy far, far away… Sorry. Wrong story. Let's begin again. It was Spring 2011 when the ghost first visited me. Almost ten years had passed since I had taken the job of Head PGA Professional at the Oakdale Golf & Country Club in California's Central Valley, and at least economically speaking, times were pretty tough for most everyone living in our little neck of the solar system. We were little more than two years into the Great Recession, and private country club membership in the U.S. had plummeted to its lowest level since shortly after the stock market crash of 1929 and the dark days of the Great Depression. Membership rolls were down more than 25 percent across the country, and nearly everyone in the golf business was struggling to adjust to financial realities not seen by anyone previously but our oldest members. At OGCC, however, despite being located in one of the five counties in the U.S. that were hardest hit, we were thriving, a proverbial island in the economic storm that had us uniquely positioned in the top 5 percent of clubs nationally. To a large degree, I was enjoying a successful tenure. I had a good staff, great members, a fair stable of successful students, and I had just been elected to my second term on the Northern California PGA's Board of Directors. At nearly every board meeting I attended, or whenever I bumped into a colleague or members from other clubs, I was being asked the same type of questions. *"How are you guys doing it?" "What's different about Oakdale?" "What's your secret?"*

It was during this prolonged period of success, however, that I became increasingly frustrated. The challenges of managing the often-overwhelming number of things required to run and remain one of the most successful facilities at the private club level had progressively swallowed my time. Time famine is something most of us are familiar with these days, and in my attempts to tame that beast, I was forever on the lookout for new tricks for efficiency that would help make sure I not only kept our uniquely successful boat afloat but also made sure we stayed ahead of the pack. Being in the golf business, I was already no stranger to 12 to 15-hour days, but despite that fact, it increasingly seemed like the only solution was to get up earlier and earlier each morning and stay at the office even later each evening. And that is when I began to be haunted by an almost daily vision—the ghost of my first boss, an embittered veteran pro who, more than 20 years previously, had spat forth what more and more had come to feel eerily like a curse.

He was on his way out the door after having been fired (coincidentally, on the very same day I had informed him I was thinking of making a career of the game) when he delivered his parting shot: "Don't even think about getting into this business if you ever want to play golf again!" At the time I gave little heed to his warning, knowing his own inability to balance work and play (both on the course and off) was the number-one reason he was on the way out. In retrospect, however, as my own level of frustration with being moved further and further away from some of the main reasons I got into the business in the first place increased, I began to understand the meaning behind his words … and that it was more than just playing golf he was talking about.

I am comforted, in a small way, by clinging to the knowledge that I am obviously not the first head golf professional to feel that way. My predecessor at OGCC left behind a golf towel printed by the PGA of America many years ago, which listed the myriad of hats that golf professionals wear daily. Tournament Coordinator, Instructor, Rules Official, Golf Shop Manager, Apparel & Equipment Buyer, Inventory Control Manager,

Committee Member, Jr. Golf Leader, and, oh, about 70 other things I won't bother to list right now. Fourteen years later it is the sole surviving thing of his in my office, serving alternately as consolation and irritation. It is consolation in the best of times, reminding me that others have figured out a way to manage this juggling act with at least some degree of success. And then, often during the same day, it is a form of metaphorical nails on a chalkboard during some of my less than productive moments— like when I'm responding to my eighth different request of the week to donate a foursome of golf. It's from the chairman of some quasi-charitable organization that is holding a fundraiser 150 miles away, who got the green light from his wife's uncle's next door neighbor, who just happens to be a member at the club. Sooooo, I need to reply.

It's the nature of the business, and at one time or another, most head golf professionals lament the lost opportunities that increased responsibility brings. Oh, to be back in the halcyon days of the assistant professional, when the luxury of less responsibility—combined with the necessities of a position that put you behind the starter's counter more often—afforded you the opportunity to spend more time daily getting to know your members and potential clients better. You heard their stories, their jokes, and their oftentimes-painful blow-by-blow descriptions of their successes and failures on the links. And you listened with a sympathetic ear and likely shared yours with them in return while offering up some potential ideas about what they could do to get better. You connected with more people, more often, more directly, and as a result you were seen as more accessible, more approachable, more outgoing, more friendly, and less intimidating than your boss.

This unfortunate disconnection is the all-too-common side effect of that increased responsibility, and as head golf professionals we either sense or hear how it affects people's perception of us, leaving us feeling at times as if people think we actually prefer the solitude of the office and the role of an administrator. We got into the business in the first place because we love the game and helping the people who play it, but more often than not we end up spending countless hours doing just about everything but that. And while we are doing necessary things (many of which can be rewarding in their own way) and things that require successful execution to ensure a club runs smoothly, they simultaneously prohibit opportunities for interaction. So at times they can seem a long way away from the things that feel the most important.

So that is where I found myself: grateful for my position and enjoying a great deal of what I was doing thanks to our success, but simultaneously wishing I could find a way to start talking the game more and hopefully find a way to reconnect. I had learned much in a near quarter century teaching, much that I wanted to share, but it's impossible to give a lesson to or play nine holes with every member (even if they were interested), and the few opportunities I had were being swallowed up by other responsibilities. I needed a new way to reach out. And that is when the idea for a weekly column hit me.

So that was my single step. I had always enjoyed writing and had a bit of experience with it in college and through writing various columns for club newsletters and a small handful of now-defunct golf publications over the years and so I felt I could use my writing ability to reach out to people. It began with a weekly column called *Tip of the Week* and the occasional remark from a member just to let me know at least someone was listening. At first they were mostly nuts 'n' bolts golf tips—things with practical application, but more often than not fairly garden variety stuff that would not have been out of place on a *Golf Digest* or *Golf Magazine* site. Useful stuff for sure, but nothing I would categorize as overly inspiring. It was a platform for relating my knowledge and for inviting people to come in and spend some time in further discussion about their potential application.

Then my father came down with cancer for the fourth time. He was getting ready to leave on an out-of-town golf trip when a nagging sore neck finally convinced him to pay a visit to the chiropractor. Ultimately that lead to his diagnosis the next day. It was not just that he came down with cancer again, but the fact that the diagnosis required an immediate risky nine-hour surgery from which there was a good chance he wouldn't wake up. The initial shock hit me pretty hard. His previous bouts with the disease seemed fairly routine, and we were all convinced he'd beat it after more than four years in remission. Now I don't need to go into the psychological ramifications of potentially losing a parent, as we can all pretty much relate to the concept whether we've been through it or not, but in this case it might have hit even a bit closer to home because of what I do for a living.

My dad was more than just another golfer; he lived for the game, and his and my mother's entire lifestyle and peer group revolved around it. It was my dad who encouraged me to play once he had resigned himself to the fact that I wasn't ultimately going to play first base for the New York Mets. And from the time I was about nine years old until I could drive, it was my dad who dropped me off most every day of every summer and most weekends at the course at sunrise and who picked me up again at dark. He was the man who gave me the opportunity and who made sacrifices so that I could play the game as much as I wanted to, and he was the man who was ultimately responsible for me staying involved with the game at a time when that wasn't necessarily a foregone conclusion. It really brought into focus life's frailty and how quickly things can change for us all, but at the same time it highlighted for me how deep many of our relationships with the game become.

Well, the next day I had a pretty hard time thinking about much of anything else and as a result I spent a good portion of that day doing two things. The first was to organize a golf trip for him, something that would inspire him to get better should he make it through the surgery. My dad grew up in upstate New Jersey, within a stone's throw of some of the most historic courses in the country, but the gates to most of those facilities weren't exactly open to the eldest son of a New York City Port

Authority Police Captain. They were blue collar, not blue blood, and as a result the closest he could have gotten to them would have been as a caddy.

One of the many great things about the game, though, is the fact that it's populated with great people. It took some clever and feverish internet searching and a few hours to find the right people, but once they heard my story, I was able to arrange a trip that would have had him walking the hallowed fairways of Baltusrol, Winged Foot, Plainfield, Garden City, and Bethpage Black (with a Mets game sandwiched in the middle for good measure), all in the span of a week. The general manager at Winged Foot was even kind enough to write a letter back to me to give to my dad, which concluded with a line saying that once he had recovered to make sure he brought his "A Game," as The Boys at Winged Foot would be waiting for him. It was a magnanimous gesture that was above and beyond anything I had hoped for, truth be told, and the consideration that I was given by all of the men who were responsible for running those facilities was one of those little things that restores your faith in humanity.

The next thing I did was to pick up my pen, so to speak. I was due to write my Tip of the Week column but didn't really feel at all like talking about the subtleties of the golf swing, the short game, putting, or anything else that I would typically write about. I was in a contemplative mood to say the least and couldn't muster even the slightest ideas for a garden-variety golf tip. I was thinking about how much Dad meant to me, how much the game meant to him, how much of an impact it had upon both of our lives, and how I knew that if one thing could inspire him down the long road to recovery, it was golf.

And then I thought about how often during my career I had seen the same thing. Golf completed people and gave their lives a sense of purpose. For some it was the competition, for others the camaraderie, and for still others it was just the routines and the exercise—something that filled the void of 40 hours worth of work they had grown accustomed to during their careers. For still others it was a vehicle to get into school (or a better school) or a means to network and do business once they had graduated. It was relaxation and relief and, for more than a few people, a necessary release that helped ensure they didn't wake up one morning and wrap their 7-iron around a boss, a co-worker, or a spouse. And for a very fortunate few, like myself, it was not just how I made my living and provided for my family, but it was truly a way of life. I guess on the surface it may seem that something like that should have been quite obvious to someone whose entire life has revolved around the game. But it suddenly became so clear to me how much more than a game the game really was. For millions around the world, for so many different reasons, it was truly a gift. And so with a sudden desire not only to thank my father for having given that gift to me but also to try and give back to the game that had given me so much, I wrote the original version of *Share the Game*.

It was a departure from my regular tip for sure, and I apologized for as much right up front. I guess I was half-expecting to be chastised for taking advantage of my soapbox to preach my own little brand of philosophy and for going all introspective at a time when I likely should have just stepped away. I had visions of people contacting me to ask to be taken off the distribution list or, worse yet, reminding me I was a golf pro, not a writer/philosopher, and that I should stick to fixing hooks and slices rather than pontificating about the game's deeper meanings. But then an even stranger thing happened...

Within hours, email after email began to fill my inbox, but instead of admonitions, they were filled with comments about how much it had touched people, how much they appreciated it, how it had reminded them of the importance of the game in their own lives or the impact of certain people who had introduced it to them, how they had passed the article on to their friends and family, and how it really made them want to share the game. I had shared something deeply personal but at the same time had apparently done so in a way that a lot of people could relate to. I had never really had that volume or kind of response to anything I had said or written before, and while to a degree (I am not ashamed to admit) it felt good to know that I had reached people, even more than that, it made me realize for the first time how powerful, when used in the right way, my words really could be.

And so there was no going back to my typical tips, back to things that you could read in nearly any golf magazine, or back to anything that I didn't really feel had at least the potential to help people with more than just the number they put down on their scorecards. It has often been said that golf is a metaphor for life, and I wouldn't be the first person to put pen to paper to try and draw the parallels, but as much as I had studied it for close to 25 years and as passionate as I had always been about helping people to improve, it was as if I was suddenly looking at the problem through a slightly different lens, and it seemed that the paths to potential solutions became just a bit clearer.

I had studied the mental side of the game for years, knowing and accepting the fact that it was the real difference between players who played at an elite level and those who didn't, but it was always in a paradigm of golf, as if the game and everything related to it sort of existed in a vacuum. As a result, I was suddenly overwhelmed with the sense that I had been approaching everything like a proverbial horse with blinkers on. The more I looked around at things people struggled with in the game, the more I seemed to see the potential solutions wouldn't likely be all that different than the solutions to problems that nearly everyone deals with in other avenues of life. It was amazingly simple, yet not so easy. Roadblocks you encountered in the game (e.g. losing your temper, inability to focus, negativity, etc.) were so often parallel to those you were encountering in the rest of your life, whether you realized it or not, and if you struggled to overcome them in another area, you weren't likely to find the going easier when it came to golf. The beauty of it, though, was that fixing or addressing a problem in one area would nearly always pay dividends in another, even if those areas weren't necessarily related.

The next thing I would have to prove, though, was a little bit tougher. People had been moved, and they paid particularly close attention when I had a serious tragedy going on in my life—but would they be so engaged once my immediate crisis had passed and I wasn't necessarily tugging at their heartstrings? I knew I couldn't really go to that well too often and that in order to keep them engaged I was going to have to not only help them and educate them, but also interest and entertain them. I love to read, and I most enjoy it if the material goes beyond mere entertainment and makes me feel as if I am just a little bit smarter and more informed or that I have learned something that will help me at some point. I was worried I might lose their attention, to an extent, but fortunately those fears for the most part turned out to be unfounded.

My next half dozen or so articles would only serve to reinforce that I was headed in the right direction, and while none of them garnered as much response as the first, they consistently drew replies, questions, or comments from readers about how they had passed it along to a friend or family member they thought it would really help. This encouraged me to continue. I was still finding my style, so to speak, and my subject matter was all over the board, but that didn't seem to matter much. People, some even as far away as Finland, consistently responded that they enjoyed reading things about the game that were a little off the beaten path and that they felt might actually help them with other things in their life, as well. It was curious to me that I had more than a few people I knew ask me in those first few months if I actually wrote the pieces or if I was copying them from somewhere else. I guess I was sort of flattered and insulted all at the same time. I was flattered because they seemed to think that the columns were so good that they must have been written by a professional, but insulted (to a degree) that they figured I couldn't possibly have written them myself.

Well, weeks turned into months, and I began to wonder how in the world I would be able to continue coming up with new things to say: new tips, new ideas, new philosophical meanderings about the game, or anything else that I could think of that would help people and keep them engaged. Fortunately, for the most part, it never happened. For in golf, as in life, there are always more lessons to be learned. And so in writing this, here is what I hope to have accomplished. On the surface, I hope you at least will find it both entertaining and educational. I obviously would love it if you came away feeling you learned at least a little something that will help your golf game, but also some things completely unrelated to the game that might cause you to pause and reflect. If I have succeeded, you may not only find some potential answers to questions that have been troubling you, but simultaneously some potentially new questions to ask yourself. Above all, however, I hope you will gain newfound perspective and a deeper appreciation for the game, what it means to you, and what it can teach us all about some of the most important subjects there are. I suppose these are lofty ambitions for a little collection of musings about an ancient game in which you hit and chase a little white ball, but ultimately if I've done what I set out to do, these aren't just lessons for the game of golf. They are lessons for a game far older. They are lessons for the game of life.

PART 1

ON FEAR, DOUBT, AND

SUFFERING

DON'T BE AFRAID TO CHANGE COURSE

"We cannot teach people anything; we can only
help them discover it within themselves."
– Galileo Galilei

Every once in a while, someone says something that seems to define a situation so perfectly that their words become immortal. Such was the case with legendary golf coach Jim Flick's now-famous quote, "Golf is 90 percent mental, and the other 10 percent is mental." Upon hearing it, most golfers who've played any length of time concede its wisdom with a knowing smile, brief chuckle, or a follow-up statement somewhat akin to, "Boy, isn't that the truth!" The clever irony in Flick's quote is only eclipsed by its nearly unquestionable accuracy, and together they combine to form a generally accepted truth. Golf is a difficult game, requiring possibly the most intricate and complex set of athletic motions in any sport to achieve even a small degree of success. That being said, for most of us, golf's greatest challenge is likely mental and the battle against oneself.

In light of this revelation and the almost universal acceptance of Mr. Flick's timeless wisdom, it is astonishing to me that most golf professionals are still stubbornly clinging to the thought that mastery of the mechanics of the golf swing is the yellow brick road to good golf. Sure, a fundamentally sound golf swing is an important component of achieving at the highest levels, but for one reason or another, most instructors today have fallen so in love with the mechanics of a well executed golf swing that they collectively seem unable to see the forest for the trees.

You cannot make any athletic motion (or any other motion, for that matter) without the thought and intention to do so originating in the brain. And while we can all concede that fact (and while a vast majority of golfers are ready to concede to the game being an incredibly mental one), we seem to be largely staying the course of focusing our collective efforts towards improvement on swing mechanics, a reality that could arguably be the biggest and most obvious reason the rate of improvement for the average golfer has remained so frustratingly low. So with that thought in mind, I believe it's time to take a look at the potential reasons for this disconnect and see if we can't find a way out of that proverbial forest.

For starters, as a proud member, I suppose I need to look in the mirror and come to terms with the fact that the **PGA** of

America could be at least partly to blame. In all of the time we spend training to teach and coach during our apprenticeship, the biggest portion of that time is focused on learning the mechanics of a fundamentally sound golf swing, while scant attention has historically been paid to the mental side of the game. Sure, there is a segment dealing with course management in the legendary **PGA Teaching Manual**, but we're talking a mere drop in the bucket when it comes to a tome so voluminous it makes the Warren Commission Report look like a brochure.

But there are bigger culprits in this conundrum, and since it is quite in vogue to blame the media for all that ails society, I shall in turn cast my aspersions in that direction. It could be reasonably argued that the *golf* media (Golf Channel, Golf magazines, tournament coverage, etc.) and its incessant focus on swing mechanics likely shoulders the biggest portion of the blame for where we now find ourselves. Whether it be the use of ultra-slow-motion cameras during tournaments to break down and point out the flaws in each player's swing at hundredth-of-a-second intervals or the litany of instructional programs and articles that focus almost entirely on swing mechanics, the golf media could be easily described as swing-obsessed, and they've been passing on that obsession for decades.

But since we're playing the "blame game" here, I might as well throw one of my heroes, Ben Hogan, under the bus, too. Some 50-plus years ago, when asked about the key to his near-robotic precision in ball-striking, he cryptically replied that he had discovered the secret to the golf swing. Ever since then, golf instructors the world over have embarked upon a proverbial "grail quest" to find out what in the world it was that Hogan was talking about. The reality is that the grace and poetry of a beautiful golf swing has a bit of a hypnotic effect, one that has long inspired fascination. If you're beset by the nagging fear that you might never get any better at this maddening game, though, there's a chance that you might be better off starting to look for Hogan's real secret, something altogether unrelated to his golf swing: how Hogan thought.

While long understood to be the real difference between good players and great players, the study and coaching of the mental side of the game has only really come into vogue in the last dozen years or so. Previously, the prevailing notion was that some golfers were just mentally tougher than others. Men like Bobby Jones, Ben Hogan, Jack Nicklaus, and Tiger Woods were just made of sterner stuff, born with a mental fortitude that us mere mortals didn't inherently possess. And up until about 25 years ago, that line of thinking was just sort of accepted without much consideration given to exactly how they thought or what about the way they thought made them so different.

Ever since the legendary Bobby Jones made the first golf instruction movie (and likely even before that), golf instructors have been fixated upon the idea of trying to teach people a legendary swing, rather than trying to help people discover what they can do to maximize the potential in their own games. Even now, nearly three decades into the era of modern sports psychology, only the most avid golfers have likely heard of men like **Dr. Bob Rotella, Dr. Joseph Parent, or Gio Valiante** (three of the most respected and in-demand mental game coaches on the men's and ladies' tours), while swing coaches like **Butch Harmon, Hank Haney, Sean Foley,** and many others have become celebrities and near-household names. If you're about to embark upon a quest for Hogan's Secret, though, and want to fight back that fear of failure, your time might be better spent seeking out one of the gentlemen in the former camp, rather than the latter.

It's funny, but it just seems to be so much easier for most of us to accept that a faulty golf swing is what is keeping us from reaching our full potential than it is to accept that it is faulty thinking and ways of thinking. "I know I could be better, if I could just get out of my own way!" is a common refrain, so why are we so afraid to take a step towards figuring out how? Is it the stigma in life that so many attach to any sort of mental problems that makes us hesitant to travel down the very road that the majority of us claim we most need to take? Or is it just the fact that we essentially don't have a very good roadmap and for the most part don't exactly know where and to whom to turn?

To find answers to these questions is a big part of why I have written this book. And it is the study of how a great many of these things, outside of the golf swing, can unlock the doors to real and sustained improvement that truly fascinates me. This is the real difference for not only successful golfers, but for successful athletes in most every other sport at every level who maximize their potential. This doesn't mean that improvements to our golf swings aren't sometimes necessary (and a good swing instructor can definitely help bring out the best in your abilities), but if you've been travelling down that road awhile to little avail, then maybe it's time to try a different route. And if all the while a creeping fear that you've reached the limits of your ability has begun to set in, then you're definitely ready. It is my true hope that this will be only the beginning of a new, exciting, and different type of journey for you. *So don't be afraid to change course* and join me, because as Albert Einstein once said, "Doing the same thing over and over again and expecting a different result is the definition of insanity." Ready to begin?

YOU CAN TEACH AN OLD DOG NEW TRICKS

"Fear is educated into us, and can,
if we wish, be educated out."
– Karl Augustus Menninger

I suppose before we truly begin this journey in earnest, it's important that I tell a little tale that will hopefully encourage a belief in your ability to make any of the changes suggested hereafter and open your mind to some new perspectives. This tale deals with the subject of fear and, most importantly, explains the reasons why you can have confidence in your ability to change and learn and why you should stop believing in the outdated notion that "you can't teach an old dog new tricks."

No matter where you go, if you ask a group of people what they believe is the most predominant human emotion, it will rarely take more than a moment before someone shouts it out. Fear. Regardless of ethnicity and where on this planet we were raised, it could be reasonably argued that we live in a culture of fear and ultimately make the majority of our decisions with the goal of maintaining our safety and security.

Fear and doubts about change and our security are powerful motivators. Fear is why many of us will spend a lifetime doing jobs we hate or in unrewarding careers. The allure of the benefits and promise of a secure retirement often easily outweigh our day-to-day displeasure with the actual work. Fear of change keeps many in a bad relationship, long after the love has faded. And fear is why you see so many negative ads during every political season. They're effective, because they seep into your brain subconsciously, filling you with doubts about the other guy and a nagging feeling that voting for him or her will somehow make you less safe.

When it comes to golf, experiencing fear while we play keeps us from having full access to our available talent and ultimately reaching our true potential. We all likely know someone who has a pretty nice-*looking* swing but who plays to a higher handicap than the aesthetics of their swing might suggest. Now I know what you're thinking, but despite the typical knee-jerk explanation for that, fear, not *sandbagging*, is more often than not the true culprit. And if we examine that likely suspect a bit more closely, I think it will help you come to understand better why we should be able to do something about it.

The majority of fears we have, unfortunately, are learned behavior. Studies involving the dreams of small children across cultures have revealed that just about the only inherent fears we have are of things like snakes, lions, tigers, and bears. These fears were programmed into us during our caveman days and are responsible for what we've come to know as the "fight or flight response," a reaction to threats to our security that is highlighted by a state of hyper-arousal induced by a cascade of hormones and adrenalin running through the body. This extra adrenalin was extremely useful back at a time when it helped us avoid being eaten by a bear or a saber-toothed tiger, but on the golf course it unfortunately is an unwelcome house guest, making it near-impossible to relax and execute that aesthetically beautiful swing we may have possessed even moments before. And the really silly part about it is that, aside from the occasional snake or alligator we might run across on courses in a few select areas of the world, most of the fears we typically experience on the golf course aren't exactly on par with any of the life-threatening sorts the fight or flight response was designed to confront. The good news is, though, we now have indisputable proof that what we have learned we can unlearn, even if we are already an extremely "old dog."

Curiously, the notion that it is significantly more difficult to train older dogs (and, by extension, older people) than younger ones has been around for a very long time. And while it may have been prevalent even earlier, the first chronicled mention of this phenomenon is in *Fitzherbert's Book of Husbandry*, printed in 1534, which contained the following passage...

> "He muste tech his dogge to barke whan he wolde haue hym, to ronne whan he wold haue hym, and to leue running whan he wolde haue hym; or els he is not a cunning shepherd. He must lerne it, whan he is a whelpe, or els it wyl not be: for it is hard to make an olde dogge to stoupe."

Fortunately, being a golf instructor, the hazards of my profession don't include having to teach anyone to *stoupe* (an outdated term for teaching a dog to put his nose to the ground to pick up a scent). I have, however, had the pleasure (or displeasure) of having many a student come to me saddled with pre-conceived notions and negative attitudes about their potential and/or inability to learn this great game or improve upon whatever game they already possess, due to their even slightly advanced age. They come armed with a litany of excuses, but a typical one I hear (particularly from those who picked the game up anywhere past about the time when they stopped believing in Santa Claus) goes something like, "Well, I didn't start playing as young as most people I know. I wish I had started a lot earlier, because I'm afraid I'm just too old to really get much better now."

Aaahh, the perception of the powers of youth. We were stronger, more flexible, more resilient, less fearful, and able to pick up new skills faster than a common cold in a daycare center full of runny-nosed three-year-olds. We had fewer doubts and were less set in our ways, less conditioned to failure, less aware of the real difficulty of things, and less afraid of the consequences of blows to our well guarded ego. At some point, however, the so-called *wisdom of age* sets in, and we become convinced that most everything we do or would do is so much harder to learn now. We long for that magically adaptive power we possessed in our younger days and that blissful ignorance of youth. It is a widely held misconception and one that seems, at one point or another, to have us all yearning to hit the proverbial reset button and turn back the clock.

Fortunately, however, there is increasing evidence that this hopeless point of view (and the resulting doubt and fear that it's too late to learn, change, and reach our ultimate potential) is for the most part unfounded. Thanks to new discoveries in brain science, we now know that we are able to learn new skills, break old habits, and overcome long-standing obstacles throughout our lives, even into our 90s. Unfortunately, however, since perception is 90 percent of reality, until people start learning the truth about this new science, they will continue to stubbornly cling to the "old dog" mentality that keeps so many people from even trying.

This relatively new science is known as neuroplasticity (or brain plasticity), a catch-all term for the changes in neural pathways and synapses that are a result of changes in behavior, environment, neural processes, thinking, emotions, and bodily injury. The discovery of the brain's ability to change and even grow throughout our lives has rapidly replaced the old model that held the brain to be a physiologically static organ; the new study of how this works has brought a great deal of hope and potential to the prospect of us acquiring new skills and improving existing ones as we age.

At this point, I suppose I could get into all the gory details of how it works (and it's actually quite fascinating research, if you're interested). But since this isn't a high school science class, I'm afraid that, if I do, a great many of you will be headed en masse for the exits (or at least turning the pages to the next chapter). Let's just say for simplicity's sake that the mounting evidence that it does work means you are no longer resigned to playing to the same 19 handicap the rest of your life, having the worst short game in your group, being the most ill-tempered, or the only one in your regular foursome whose sudden case of the yips has you doomed to a long, dark future of standing over every two-foot putt with all the steadiness of a plate full of Jell-O.

Under the old brain model, after a certain age, we would have essentially been "stuck" with faulty patterns of thought that involve doubt, fear, wild mood swings, and an inability to stay focused or pick up new skills. Armed with a basic understanding of the science of neuroplasticity, we can now begin to develop new ways to eliminate or change these faulty patterns of thought with the confidence that the new ones can successfully replace the old, as long as we are willing to put the time and effort into learning to retrain them.

Now, whether you were aware of your brain's ability to change and learn or not, I suppose at this point you are most likely thinking, *That's great. I'm glad that even my little pea-brain has such massive potential for growth, but how do I actually go about training it?* Well, I would give you a number of places to start and, after some analysis, would come up with a customized program based upon your individual challenges if you were a student of mine, but in the absence of that immediate reality, I think the best thing I can do to get you started is turn you over to another group of professionals.

THINQ Golf is an organization that has come about as a collaboration of a few sports psychologists, neuroscientists, and PGA/LPGA professionals who wanted a set of tools to help develop the mental game skills needed in golf based upon the concept of neuroplasticity. Their iPhone app has a series of different science-based games and a variety of mental training exercises that have been designed to help make your brain more "synchronous," which is the major difference noted when studying the brain maps of elite athletes and those of amateurs. These games are a pretty fun and easy way to pass some of that downtime in the waiting room at the dentist's office or elsewhere, which you might currently be filling with a few levels of *Angry Birds* or rounds of *Words with Friends*, and they can actually help you improve your own brain in areas like attention, adaptability, awareness, intention, and synchronicity. You can check it out at thinqgolf.com.

In the end, the science of neuroplasticity has proven that we have the ability to grow, change, and learn throughout our lives, which is enough to get us started and can be an amazingly liberating and exciting prospect as we age. In the golf world, this translates to the fact that "you *can* teach an old dog new tricks," a fact that should leave us all with newfound hope that, if our golf game really isn't up to the level of where we aspire to play, we have the ability to make the necessary changes that will help us reach heights we might have previously thought unattainable. And while that knowledge alone doesn't guarantee success, it should at least inspire us to get started without the burden of that age-old fear of being just too much of an *old dog*.

KILL YOUR COMFORT ZONE

"Verily the lust for comfort murders the passion of the soul, and then walks grinning into the funeral."
– Khalil Gibran

As you've likely guessed by now, I am a great collector of quotes and love how the timeless wisdom of very memorable ones can serve to repeatedly impact our decision-making over time. Each morning on the way to school, my daughters and I engage in a little exercise that I like to call *words of wisdom,* where I relate a famous quote to them and we talk about what it means and how it would apply to their lives. Every staff meeting I hold ends with a famous quote that is topical to the day's discussion, and I file each and every one for use at a later date. Even with as large of a collection as I have, every now and then I come across a new one that really stays with me and serves as a recurring reminder of virtues I truly value. So it was with this one, and while it can be applied to a myriad of facets of life, when it comes to golf, for me it really serves to highlight how our fears create a near-desperate attachment to our "comfort zones," which can very often be the linchpin to our problems in reaching "The Zone."

You've heard of the "The Zone," that Holy Grail that athletes in nearly every sport search for, as it holds a near-magical elixir of exceptional performance. Golfers of nearly every level have at least tasted it, even if only briefly. It is that elusive stretch of holes or rounds (less common) where we can seemingly do no wrong. Drives fly farther, approaches straighter, and the hole looks as big as bucket. You play with a sense of quiet confidence, as if you've finally discovered the key to making the game easy, and for at least a fleeting moment, you're teased with the idea that it will be forever yours to hold. As we all know, however, it is merely a mirage, and like that imagined desert oasis, it is an illusion that fades from view nearly as quickly as it appeared. When the game is your passion, though, you don't give up easily, and once we've tasted it, many of us will spend a near-lifetime trying desperately to get back there.

Your "comfort zone," on the other hand is a place that is easily found. It's one you inhabit on a day-to-day, round-to-round basis, and it is a place innate forces seem to pull you inexorably back to whenever you step just beyond it to taste the tantalizingly sweet nectar of "The Zone." You par three holes in a row, only to follow them up with two double-bogeys. You hit your best drive in a year, setting yourself up for a short wedge to a vulnerable pin, and you dump it into the bunker. You knock your approach stone dead, two and a half feet from the pin, only to walk up and make a quick yippy little stab at the ball that slides by the hole without even touching the cup. We've all done something like it before and then walked away frustrated, muttering to ourselves, possibly applying something a bit short of love to the offending club, or pitching the stupid ball into a nearby lake. It's comfortable but unfortunately familiar territory. A place where we are continually reminded of how much more we would be capable of if we could just stay out of our own way long enough to reach our true potential.

Well, truth be told, even Tour players deal with similar issues. And while on the surface it sure appears their comfort zones are a lot closer to The Zone, it doesn't feel any different and isn't any easier for them than it is for us. And the first step we all need to take to get beyond it is often the most difficult. Our comfort zones are places where we can typically control the outcomes and we understand the expectations. Whether we want to admit it or not, this lust for comfort is something our brains have been overtly conditioned to crave almost since birth, and moving beyond our comfort zone is by definition uncomfortable and unfamiliar. Our family, friends, and society encourage us to go along and get along, to conform and acclimate, to blend and behave, and ultimately do nothing that will make us stand out or embarrass those same friends, family members, or ourselves. As much as we celebrate and reward stand-outs and individuality as a culture with our Hollywood stars, our sports heroes, and our *American Idol*s, behind the scenes the pursuit of such frivolity and more lofty ambitions is commonly discouraged, as we are steered towards more realistic goals and the safer path of the four-year degree, the steady job, and the security of a comfortable yet modest retirement.

Despite all that, however, I'm here to tell you that you can defy years and even decades of conditioning, but if you want to get beyond your comfort zone, then you might just need to kill it! The formula for doing this may not look exactly the same for everyone, but to get started you need to do so by doing those things that you instinctively avoid the most. Sign up for Speechmasters if your fear is public speaking, sign up for open mic night at a local coffee house, or even audition for a part in a local production. Go bungee jumping, skydiving, or rock-climbing if you have a fear of heights and look down, intentionally and repeatedly. Afraid of flying? Book a flight somewhere, anywhere, but preferably somewhere you actually would like to go. The smaller the plane, the better. And if you just can't stand standing out, do something that will make people take notice. Dance down the street without any apparent music, lie down for a quick rest in a crowded public place, or do any other silly embarrassing act you can think of that won't immediately land you in jail, get you fired from your job, or have your relatives scrambling for the phone number of the guys in the white coats.

As far as your golf game goes, you can start with changing your on-course demeanor. If you're the quiet introvert, forever silently stewing or brooding over that last missed putt, then make a pact to engage your fellow playing partners. Ask them about their families, their work, or their recent trips. If you're the veritable Mount Vesuvius in your group, always on the verge of an eruption, make a concentrated effort to truly laugh at every missed shot (and your past behavior) and make certain your clubs' only "air time" is while they're still attached to your hands during the act of a swing. And if you're the life of your foursome, always ready with a new joke or story, eternally distracted and distracting while you're waiting for the next opportunity to speak, try going a hole or two focused only on your next shot, offering nothing more than a polite "you're away" to your buddies and watch to see what their reaction is.

The reality is that stepping beyond your comfort zone in one area—any area—can have amazing benefits, and when it comes to golf, it will very likely get you a little closer to finding The Zone on a more regular basis than you ever thought possible as you get more and more comfortable with feeling a bit of fear and uneasiness on a regular basis. And as far as life goes? Well, chances are you'll end up reawakening that passion in your soul and feeling more alive than you have in quite a long time. So *kill your comfort zone* by confronting those things that have been holding you back, and make a habit of putting yourself into places or acting in ways that make you feel at least a little bit fearful and less than comfortable. It's never as bad or as hard as you worry it will be, and you will grow in so many ways that when all is said and done and it's time for the ol' pine box, I'll venture to bet you'll be the one left grinning.

USE DOUBT TO FUEL YOUR DRIVE

"I love it when people doubt me. It makes me
work that much harder to prove them wrong."
– Derek Jeter

When it comes to the sports world, it is generally accepted that there are those who are clutch performers and those who aren't. The acceptance of this idea is deeply embedded in our sports culture and in the game of golf in particular. There is a particular problem with this line of thought, however. It isn't true. Yes, you heard me right, and no, I haven't completely lost my marbles. There is no such thing as a clutch performer.

For most of us, when I say *clutch*, the images that come to mind are of legendary atheletes like Larry Bird, Derek Jeter, Joe Montana, and of course Tiger Woods—men who rose to the occasion in moments of intense pressure and consequence and whose performance during those moments seemed to not only match their day-to-day feats, but exceed them. The bigger the moment, the higher they seemed to rise, and the more clutch they became.

There is a wealth of new research out there, however, that disputes everything we have come to believe about athletes and their ability to perform under pressure. Analyzing study after study about the amygdala (the brain's fear center) and how it works, as well as exhaustive amounts of statistics in nearly every sport at the highest level, scientists have come to a conclusion. There is no such thing as a clutch athlete, and there has never been a player documented in any sport who has ever consistenly risen above his or her regular level of performance in pressure-filled situations.

Yes, even the best players of all time, names like the ones mentioned above, do not have levels of performance in the biggest games, matches, or tournaments that are measurably different than what they displayed on the average day. They do, however, all have one thing in common. They don't choke! It is not that they play any better than they do normally, but they generally don't play any worse. Our sports culture, without realizing it, has come to actually revere those who can play under the pressure of the biggest moments without their level of performance taking a step backwards, while silmultaneously believing in the myth of the clutch performer. The somewhat humorous revelation behind this is that we have unwittingly come to revere merely average performances, due to our expectation and acceptance of the fact that the majority of athletes will almost naturally choke once the heat is on.

The problem when it comes to competitive golf is that this pervasive expectation that intense doubts and fear will sabotage most men's games becomes a self-fulfilling prophecy. We expect to be anxious in big situations, and we expect that only a handful of unique individuals that are born with an innate ability to block out that fear or rise above it (or who don't actually even feel it) will ever succeed. If you do a little research on the matter, however, you will find that even the most clutch performers feel and have felt nervoussness, doubts, and fear during their biggest moments. Bill Russell used to throw up just prior to every game, Dennis Eckersley was so scared he used false cockiness and bravado to hide it from his opponents, and Michael Jordan would use statements from reporters, opponents, or opposing coaches to work up enough anger to outweigh the anxiety.

The difference between those iconic athletes and those who choke is how their brains processed doubt and fear during those crucial moments and what they *didn't* do. They didn't allow it to scare them. Instead, they used it to motivate themselves and as a reminder of the fact that their ability had put them in exactly the place they wanted to be. They came to define that nervous energy as more excitement than anything. And under no circumstances did they allow themselves to develop sudden irrational doubts about their ability to perform or overanalyze or even pay much attention to the mechanics of their given skill.

So in a nutshell, those who seem to rise to the occasion have learned to use their doubts and fears in ways that benefit them and motivate them to perform and succeed. They keep their minds focused outward, on those that doubt them, how they plan to prove them wrong, the specifics of the task at hand, or on the process to do all of that, rather than inward, where it can grow into doubts about their specific abilities. Because in truth, we all feel doubt and fear from time to time, but if you can learn to *use doubt to fuel your drive* and not allow it to change your belief in yourself and what you are capable of doing out there, you will be a lot less apt to choke. And as a result, you just might end up being the one everybody else thinks is clutch.

JUST GO AWAY!

"I've known a great many troubles in life, most of which have never actually happened."

– Mark Twain

Mark Twain is one of the most quotable men in American literature and he—not surprisingly, given the self-deprecating nature of a good many of the quotes attributable to him—played a bit of golf in his leisure time. Being a golfer (at least a dedicated one) far too often means we have become masters at putting ourselves through a great deal of mental suffering, so you need to also develop a healthy sense of humor and the ability to laugh at yourself to get through it.

We can hit a great shot, hit the pin, and have the ball carom back into a bunker or lake. At the same time, some of us will receive the benefit of the *member's bounce*—that horrible shot everyone hits at one time or another that strikes a branch, a cart path, or a sprinkler head and kicks back in play, onto the green, or even occasionally into the hole (by law the last one only happens to people that have been playing the game for less than a month). We strive to improve yet are reluctant to change, bringing to mind Einstein's previously mentioned definition of insanity. We stand upon the first tees of the world, palms sweating, collars tightening, and heart rates rising, while visions of imagined wayward shots and the disapproving looks from all who stand nearby dance wildly through our heads. We worry and hurry through our rounds, cursing and throwing our clubs, sometimes even into a nearby lake, then swear off the game for good (for the third time this month), only to sneak back that night in hopes of retrieving the offending articles. It's just a game, we say, yet at times it's an emotional rollercoaster, careening out of control while leaving our outlook on life itself in a state of flux from shot to shot. And though on the surface this tragicomedy appears a result of how we play, it is in truth a reflection of what is playing out in the theater of our minds.

Being in our own heads too much is one of the biggest problems for golfers at just about every level. We stand upon the tee, nervously peering down a fairway wider than a football field, and see nothing but the bunkers, the water, the deep rough, or the trees ominously lining each side. We've already mentally signed the scorecard for that 68 we're going to shoot after starting with a birdie on the first or we're so preoccupied with a four-putt double-bogey that we've made two more doubles before we wake up from the self-imposed purgatorial trance. And all this foreshadowing and rumination is neatly sandwiched in between a fair amount of self-flagellation for every errant shot and cursing at the hands of the Golf Gods for their intervention in every less-than-perfect bounce or break. It's a habitual ritual that each of us plays out to one degree or another each time we play and one that has a very direct impact upon how we score and interact with those we are with out there. And in the end, it is this ritual way of being that often invisibly anchors us and our games to a certain level of play. That is why it is a big part of what needs to change in order for us to get to that elusive next level.

So while there is often a realization amongst golfers in general that they are their own worst enemy, there is very little in the way of a generally recognized roadmap for helping you to find your way out of your own head once you've taken that fork in the road. We make our way around the course enacting this series of almost unconscious but well rehearsed routines—ones so habitual that they clear the mental space necessary for us to engage in all the aforementioned foreshadowing, rumination, and other detrimental behavior. Sure, we've all heard about how we're supposed to stay in the present, but connecting the dots from that generally recognized principle to a series of steps that you can actually take to do just that is something much less obvious and not the kind of advice you'll likely receive from your garden variety golf instructor. So in the interest of not being garden variety, I'd like to give you a few things to try the next time you find yourself seemingly mired in the swamps of your own head. The key is change, and by forcing yourself to consciously do that, you can disrupt the patterns of action and thought that ultimately result in you doing the same thing over and over again.

Step #1. Try being an extrovert. Or an introvert if you're already the outgoing type. We each have our social comfort zones and personality types that we inhabit both on and off the course, and how we interact with others is often one elaborate routine that we unknowingly engage in. To get present, we need to disrupt those well rehearsed routines by being different. Introverts need to actually talk to their playing partners and make a point of remembering their names if it's your first round together. Already outgoing? Time to shut up already. Your playing partners have already heard the story (many times) about how you knocked it stiff on No. 18 into a two-club wind last fall to take down the five-time Club Champion, so listen to their stories for once or take a look around, absorbing the scenic beauty of the course as if you were playing it for the first time.

Step #2. Stop sleepwalking. Or sleep driving, if that is the case. Offer to be the scorekeeper, if you aren't normally, and challenge yourself to remember each and every shot of all your playing partners. And at the end of the hole, rather than asking what they took, say something like, "Nice par, Jim!" And if the self-appointed scorecard czar in your group won't give it up? Keep your own. It'll be useful in the next exercise and isn't a bad thing to have anyway, in case the bets don't quite add up the way you thought they should when you're settling up in the 19th hole afterwards.

Step #3. Track your ability to stay present. This is another good reason to be the scorekeeper and is a mindful awareness practice borrowed from the world of Zen Buddhism. Place two columns on your scorecard—one titled past and the other titled future. Without beating yourself up about it, just make a little mental note during the play of each hole when your mind wanders to something in the future (like that 68 you're going to shoot) or something in the past (like that stupid little three-footer you missed for birdie four holes ago), and note them on the card at the end of the hole. The practice of just noticing and making a note of when your attention drifts, without reacting to it, is known as *non-judgmental awareness*. And while the explanation for why this awareness can help break you of the habit is a bit of a long and winding road to go down at the moment, at present just trust me and accept it on faith because it has been successfully used for millennia to do just that.

Now please understand that this is just a beginning. All change needs to start somewhere, and making these three little mental disciplines a part of your new routine can be the start of developing a new you. A new you that might surprise your playing partners not only with a difference in demeanor, but with a different golf game, as well. Being different requires you to be in the moment, essentially forcing you to stay in the present rather than in your own head. You may not ultimately decide that the new you is for you, but forcing the old you to *just go away*, even if it is only for a little while, might be all you need to do to stop suffering in your own head long enough to learn the process of staying in the here and now. After all, while golf is a great game, if we can't learn to appreciate everything it has to teach us, we can easily turn what could be the greatest game into Mark Twain's proverbial "good walk spoiled."

AS A MAN THINKETH SO IS HE

"The mind is everything. What you think you become."
– Gautama Buddha

For some reason the words suffer and golf seem inexorably intertwined. Now I'm not talking about suffering of biblical proportions, like that of Job, the Jews in Egypt, or Chicago Cubs fans, but the type derived from punishing self-directed words, thoughts, and emotions—a type most golfers seem all too familiar with. That quote from Buddha was supposedly uttered almost 2,500 years ago. And so while that was at least a couple of thousand years before modern golf was invented by the Scots, that statement is so applicable to the game that I would swear (not on the Bible, of course) that old Gautama must have at least been familiar with *Chuiwan*, the primitive form of the game that scholars now say originated in China around that time.

It should be an obvious thing to avoid, but it is amazing how many people who play golf talk to themselves on the course in a very negative way. *Chump, hacker, duffer,* and *choker* are words in every golfer's lexicon and ones that are far too often self-directed. Your brain is amazingly receptive to the power of suggestion. This is why hypnosis is so effective on so many people. What your brain repeatedly hears, it will soon begin to believe, and while there is a steady drip of brain chemicals at work that explain scientifically what happens when we hear an unending barrage of self-directed negativity, for the sake of simplicity, let's just say your thoughts control your mood. Literally. And if you are in the habit (or trap) of constantly talking to yourself in a way that is less than positive, you will ultimately adopt that as part of your identity, and your mood will never be primed to play your best golf.

So let's take a quick look at some of the bad habits of thought most negative self-talkers suffer from and a little something they might be able to do to change.

1. Catastrophizing. Most negative self-talkers are masters at looking at any given situation and distilling it down to only the negative possible outcomes. It may be difficult at first, but you need to accept that at least some good can come from nearly every situation, even if it's only a lesson to be learned, and just because you hit a branch no bigger than your pinky finger 200

yards away that kicked your ball O.B. right off the first tee, it is no reason to slump your shoulders and exclaim, "Here we go again. Stick a fork in me. This round's done!" Again.

2. Personalizing. Negative self-talkers have a hard-wired need to blame themselves for everything that goes wrong. Bad breaks are bad breaks, bad bounces are just bad bounces, and bad luck is exactly what it is, not some karmic hand of the universe reaching down to punish you for that piece of Halloween candy you stole from your sister back in the third grade.

3. Polarizing. Everything is too often black and white, wrong or right, or good or evil for those in the habit of self-flagellation and there is no gray area. Consider the wisdom of Buddha's "Middle Way" and the fact that you, your game, or the next round doesn't have to be blissfully bogey-free in order for it not to be a total disaster. I've been witness to more than a few course records being broken over the years, and not even one of them was accomplished without at least one bad hole.

Proverbs 23:7 says, "As a man thinketh so is he!" And while those words weren't written quite as long ago as Buddha's, it should be obvious by now that the ancients had something figured out long ago that many of us are still struggling to accept. What you think, you will ultimately become. So whether it's on the golf course, the tennis court, in the boardroom, or anywhere else in life, make a pact with yourself to stop suffering from this type of talk. Remember that each hole is a new hole, each round a new round, and (as long-suffering Cubs fans can attest) each new spring is a golden opportunity to begin the quest anew, as long as we train ourselves to think of it that way. I'm not saying that freeing yourself from the limitations of negative self-talk will guarantee you'll be angling for the **PGA** or **LPGA** Tour anytime soon, but I am guaranteeing that it will make it a whole lot easier for you to play your best game and to start enjoying yourself on the course and elsewhere a whole lot more.

PART 2

ON ANGER,

FRUSTRATION, AND

IRRITATION

TEMPER YOUR TEMPER

"A quick temper will make a fool of you soon enough!"
– Bruce Lee

It is often said that golf builds character. While I believe this to be true, there is one thing that I can say for sure—golf definitely *reveals* character. Fairly often, I have to work with very talented young students on learning to control their tempers and how to mitigate the fallout from those occasional emotional outbursts. Well, unfortunately, those foolish episodes aren't necessarily confined to the young and immature but are often witnessed in players of every age in the form of thrown and broken clubs, divots and unnecessary damage to the course, as well as the types of audible displays of anger that leave the rest of one's foursome wishing they were playing in another group. Sometimes these little fits are in reaction to not playing up to our own expectations, and other times it is because of what we perceive as the perpetual bad breaks that the golf gods seem to be sending our way. And still other times, they are a manifestation of things in our lives off the course and unfortunately spill out during moments of extreme frustration.

It doesn't necessarily have to be that way, and for starters, a little change of perspective can go a long way towards breaking this cycle of anger and frustration and not only winning more golf tournaments, but winning back a few of our playing partners that we may have alienated. Jack Nicklaus once won a tournament at Doral in which, after a perfect drive on the closing hole, he ended up in a divot. After taking a little extra time surveying the shot, he calmly hit the ball on the green and two-putted for par to win by a shot. After the round the press immediately asked him about the obvious bad break on 18, and he responded by saying, "Actually, that bad lie may have been fortunate because it forced me to focus on staying down through the shot." Instead of getting frustrated and using his perceived bad break as an excuse, he turned it into an advantage. That's the type of player I like to coach and one that I think everyone enjoys playing with.

Another pitfall to be avoided and which often leads to these unfortunate episodes is elevated expectations that aren't necessarily in line with our ability. "Expect less and get more" is a common saying, and it is particularly helpful when it comes to avoiding frustration and the inevitable outbursts that seem to go hand-in-hand with a player whose perception of their game isn't quite in line with their actual game. In this situation I like to turn to a story I once heard about a PGA professional who had an exceptionally talented young student who was prone to fits of anger when he missed more than a couple of greens in regulation or shot scores even a little over his expectation. Frustrated with his inability to get through to the student, he assigned him the task of going to the local PGA Tour event and following around Dave Stockton.

After doing so for a single round, he came back incredulous, saying, "You won't believe it—that guy Stockton only hit six greens all day. I hit that many in nine holes!"

"Did he lose his temper, slam his club into the ground, or show any other outward sign of frustration when he missed a green?" asked the pro.

"No," said the junior player.

"And so what did he shoot?"

"Sixty-nine, and he just acted the entire time like that's the way you're supposed to play!"

"Well, now you have seen a real golfer!" said the pro.

I'm not saying that you can't display a little frustration from time to time while you are on the course. For some it is undeniably a necessary release. But if you seem to be having a tough time finding your game these days (or even finding a game), you might want to take an honest look at yourself and the potential foolishness of your behavior while you're out there. Imagine what you would think if you witnessed that same display or pattern of behavior in one of your playing partners or, worse yet, your children. If it's something you wouldn't be proud of, then maybe it's time to *temper your temper*. It will be beneficial in the battle to play your best golf and make you a much better example when the eyes of our future generation are focused your way; commit to it, and you just might start getting a few more golfing invitations, as well.

LAUGH IN THE FACE OF FRUSTRATION

"Against the assault of laughter nothing can stand."
– Mark Twain

When it comes to golf and the idea of playing better golf, aside from a handful of clever quotes that have been passed down over the years, laughter isn't a subject that I believe has been given its proper due. In truth, I'm not sure it has been given any due at all, so I would like to be the first pro to go on record as saying that laughter not only is the most untapped resource each of us possesses, but also could very well be every golfer's secret weapon. Yes, that's right. A well timed snicker, chortle, or chuckle just might be even more powerful than a bagful of the latest and most technologically advanced equipment. Now I realize calling laughter a weapon might bring up images of Maxwell Smart and his litany of faux-cool gadgets like the shoe gun or the laser blazer, but stick with me because the really funny part is that the majority of golfers have no idea they are even in possession of a weapon of such magnitude, let alone how and when to use it.

Golf can be cruel. Not only is acquiring the skill to hit a golf ball both long and straight a nearly herculean task, it is a game whose playing field is beset with traps and pitfalls designed to snare even the most slightly awry attempts. Throw in the ever-present possibility for bad breaks, bumps, and bounces, and you have a game that can at times seem nearly sadistic in its design. This is where the ability to laugh in the face of adversity can become an asset; however, it is an ability that seems nearly absent in the majority of players. Thrown clubs, broken clubs, expletive-laced tirades, sulking, and minor temper tantrums (of the sort I sometimes witness from my six-year-old) are the most common reactions you see to the invariable pitfalls the game present us. And even the best players in the world aren't seemingly immune, as we've witnessed golfers like Tiger Woods kick one of his clubs on camera or Rory McIlroy even throw one into a nearby lake in response to a shot that came off less than his expectations. Thankfully, there is an alternative.

Laughter has long been called the best medicine, and upon finding actual medical evidence to support this belief in many studies, Dr. Madan Kitaria wrote an article declaring such in 1995 and had an epiphany. He started the first known laughter club in Mumbai, India, which combined laughter, meditation, and yogic breathing to help one achieve a state of unconditional joyfulness that is independent of circumstances. This may sound silly, and Kitaria said as much when he first came up with the idea, figuring people would have initially laughed at him if he hadn't been a doctor. Despite the almost laughable idea, they were quickly successful, and laughter clubs began springing up all around the globe, with about 2,500 in existence today. Scientific evidence has found that laughter decreases stress hormones and has actual analgesic benefits. Combine this with laughter's ability to increase the heart rate more than aerobic exercise, and you have a near-magic bullet in the battle to combat stress and create joyfulness. Collectively these elements provide the body and mind with a whole host of benefits that are invaluable in both golf and life. If you want to find out more specifically, check out laughteryoga.org.

O.K., I'm sure that sounds nice and all, but let's circle back to the concept of how laughter can be used to help improve our golf. The human brain has a complex retrieval structure, but for the sake of simplicity, let's just say that you have a far greater ability to retrieve good thoughts, memories, feelings, and emotions when you are in a good mood. This is where laughter becomes so valuable. It lightens our mood and puts us in the optimal frame of mind to recall successes and quickly put failures behind. Sure, the ability to laugh at oneself is an admirable quality and useful in many areas of life, but being able to call on that ability at will is something that can literally change your game. The moments immediately following a shot, especially a poor shot, are some of the most difficult in the game, and that's where laughter can become your secret weapon.

Noted sports psychologist and golf coach **Dr. Glen Albaugh** invented a clever post-shot routine that helps to manage this period fairly effectively, and it is used by numerous tour players. However, in light of all that I have just mentioned, it is absent one key ingredient. Laughter. Not the barely audible chuckle or the self-deprecating false laughter some players employ instinctively, but genuine laughter—the laughter of children that is completely devoid of self-consciousness. It might feel fake at first, but once you learn how to do it, understand how truly beneficial it is, and stop worrying what other people think, it will start to feel more and more real until it really is. So the next time you slice one into the woods, don't break your club or curse and swear. *Laugh in the face of frustration*, and not only will you feel better faster, but you just might find that you stop letting that one bad shot turn into three bad holes.

MAKE YOUR SIGNATURE MOVE

"Good habits formed during youth make all the difference."
– Aristotle

Every semester in my Acorn Academy classes, I like to give all of our young students a homework assignment. Develop a signature move. *What is a signature move?* you might ask. Well, for simplicity's sake, let's just say it is something akin to the saber-rattling move Chi Chi Rodriguez used to make after he dropped a particularly significant putt or Tiger Woods's iconic fist-pump. The kids really get a kick out of it, especially when I ask them to make a short putt and then perform it in front of the class. When we do it, however, I never fail to notice the half-concerned and somewhat puzzled looks I receive from the casual onlookers and even some of the parents who are camped out just beyond the edges of the putting green. So before you all go and worry that I'm teaching our younger generation to become a bunch of hot-dogging, fist-pumping, *you-da-man*-shouting obnoxious bores out on the golf course, let me assure you there is more to this than mere entertainment value, and there is certainly a method to my madness.

Golf can be a frustrating game at times, depending upon your perspective and the habits you have developed because of it. We are all creatures of habit of one form or another, and the all-too-common habit among many golfers is to get upset, moan, complain, curse, throw clubs, break clubs, and generally act like some sort of Oakland Raiders fan after every missed shot or putt. The game itself sets us up for this to a degree because (by design) we fail far more than we succeed. And for some reason, the game simultaneously seems to attract more than its fair share of perfectionists who expect an unrealistically high degree of success on every shot. You know the type—the guy or gal who lives under the curious belief that if they react strongly enough to every slightly missed shot or putt, they will convince everyone in a three-county area that if it weren't for the planets being out of alignment or some other mysterious forces conspiring against them, they would have easily turned that 92 into a 68!

I'm going to let you in on a little secret. Your brain has a fascinating little habit of remembering in much greater detail and more easily recalling situations and events that are tied to your strongest feelings of emotion. So if you are in the habit of emotionalizing every bad shot and treating your few fleeting moments of success as ho-hum events, it won't be very long until the only thing you can recall when you're standing over the ball is every shank, chunk, top, skull, or yipped three-footer you've made since first picking up a club at the age of eight! Recognize anyone in the above description? Recognize yourself? Well, if you do, then maybe you can now see why I am teaching the kids early on the habit of celebrating their successes (in a reasonable fashion) and emotionalizing those few really good shots they make every round, while simultaneously encouraging them to develop a process for mentally throwing out the bad ones.

So if you're in the habit of reacting negatively to all those missed shots rather than celebrating the good ones, then maybe it's time you came up with a signature move. I'm not saying you need to come up with golf's version of Kaepernicking, but even a small gesture of satisfaction (performed consistently) can start the mental ball rolling in the right direction and help your brain start to erase the flood of negative mental images that succeed only in making you nervous, anxious, and irritable. And once you've got it down, be ready with it the next time you hit a good shot or drop a clutch putt and make your signature move. You might feel a little silly at first if it's not already your habit, but not half as silly as you feel when you have to explain to the pro why you need to get your putter re-shafted for the fourth time this year!

BECOME MESMERIZED, NOT HYPNOTIZED

"We cannot solve our problems with the same thinking we used when we created them."
– Albert Einstein

Some beliefs and perceptions are so long-held, commonly accepted, and generally unquestioned that we tend to either forget their origins (if we knew them to begin with) and reason for being. In all but certain circles of academia, this is the case with mesmerism and more specifically the word *mesmerized*. Many people likely think it is just another word for being hypnotized or entranced, and we might even mentally picture a gold watch swinging slowly back and forth in front of a subject wearing a far-away gaze as the practitioner, likely a man in black coattails, a monocle, and a handlebar moustache, repeats something like, "You're getting sleepy, very sleepy." This scene is typically followed by the subject being commanded to act like a monkey, quack like a duck, or do any number of things that are either somewhat silly or completely out of character. The two words, *mesmerized* and *hypnotized*, have become nearly interchangeable in our language and popular culture, yet most of us are unaware that the word mesmerized actually comes from Dr. Franz Mesmer, the German physician who advanced the theory of animal magnetism in the 1700s, ultimately laying the foundation for what has become known as the modern practice of hypnosis.

Both modern hypnosis and mesmerism have been (falsely) credited with giving their practitioners incredible power over people, due in part to the fact that those affected have historically been caused to act and behave either foolishly or at least differently than they would normally and to be able to overcome illnesses and obstacles that they couldn't otherwise. In reality, however, when you take a closer look at mesmerism and what modern hypnotists actually claim to do, it is quite different than the stereotypical Hollywood depictions that most of us have come to accept, and it is in some ways far more impressive. Since the time of Mesmer, who died in 1815, hypnosis has evolved to become one of the more effective methods to help people get over problems or bad habits that seem to stubbornly resist their best efforts and applied willpower. The reason that it works, however, as originally concluded by a panel of scientists put together by France's King Louis XVI (which interestingly included none other than Benjamin Franklin) to investigate the validity of animal magnetism, has essentially little to do with the hypnotist, but rather with the strong beliefs of the person being hypnotized.

The human mind is incredibly powerful, and under hypnosis many people's self-limiting beliefs can be stripped away so much so that they can finally see themselves for who they truly are. For the most part, since a very early age, we all have built up beliefs about ourselves, who we are, what we can or cannot do, and who we can become. Unfortunately, these beliefs can essentially become the bars of a cage that jails us. Some of these beliefs are passed on to us from our parents, teachers, friends, mentors, and other influential people that we're exposed to; however, still others are derived from our successes, failures, and other significant experiences. And very often these beliefs are so deeply held that they, rather than any real obstacle, keep us from successfully making the improvements in our lives that we so desperately wish for. In many cases they will keep us from even trying. These beliefs are, in and of themselves, a form of self-hypnosis that a great majority of us live out the majority of our lives in. This is why it is not uncommon for many hypnotists to claim what they actually do is *de*-hypnotize people.

Now the game of golf and improving your game is to an extent similar to improving any other element of your life. Before you can or would even be willing to take the first steps toward making any kind of improvement, you have to change your thinking and really believe that you can improve. You must be truly able to see and imagine yourself as being better than you are or you won't bother to try. We all likely know someone who plays the game at a certain level and it seems that they have played at that same level for years, even though they play and practice all the time. They say they want to improve, they constantly buy the newest and latest equipment, and they may even take lessons from one pro after another in search of a better game, yet their scores seem to remain the same regardless of the changes in swing or equipment they make or the amount of practice they embark upon.

This player has often, unbeknownst to them and despite their protestations, actually become comfortable with who and where they are. They identify with the level they play to and have inwardly resigned themselves to being that type of player, despite all of the outward actions that would seem to speak to the contrary. Growing requires stepping out of their comfort zone, and the unfamiliarity and uneasiness they feel during those brief moments when they actually do is their brain's way of bringing them back. It's sort of like carrying a hidden anchor—a hidden, but very real anchor that keeps them from growing and achieving their stated goals regardless of how passionately they protest.

So if you're frustrated, and struggling to improve in anything, the obvious next question is, *What can you do to get to where you say you really want to go?* Well, the first step in that journey is often to take a deeper look inward. Start seeing yourself for who you truly are and what long-held beliefs, in truth, are keeping you from becoming who you want to be. Players who possess self-limiting beliefs are typically very hard on themselves when they make mistakes and can often have a poor self-image. Regardless of how well they hit the ball on the range, they stand over it once they get on the course and proceed to imagine all of the potentially awful shots they could hit and the shame and embarrassment it will cause them once they do—not to mention the terrible sense of disappointment for succumbing to those same thoughts yet again. They have trouble letting go of bad shots, often convinced that only by dwelling on them with an appropriate amount of self-punishment can they really get better, because after all, settling for anything less than perfection leads to mediocrity. And it is because of all this self-flagellation and the accompanying feelings of frustration that they rarely feel truly comfortable over the ball, let alone confident. In fact, in many situations they can even devolve into a sense of full-blown panic!

In the end, the somewhat harsh reality is that you will never be able to really take that first step in becoming confident until you can begin to see all of the self-criticism and the accompanying anxiety and frustration for what they are. They are nothing more than warped, distorted, overly negative, and inaccurate opinions of yourself combined with the imagined opinions of others, which lead you to believe in an image of yourself that is often short of reality and far short of what you can truly become. So if you want to take that first step and begin to grow, you need to question every one of your long-held, overly jaded opinions of yourself and at the same make sure you have not allowed yourself to become inadvertently hypnotized by them. Instead, try becoming mesmerized by images of your true potential, a potential so unlimited that it opens the door to forming entirely new opinions about who and what you are and, as a result, what type of player you can ultimately become. The new discoveries about the brain and neuroplasticity that I mentioned earlier have proven it's possible— and that you really can move beyond the age-old problems this type of thinking creates. You just can't do it with the same old type of thinking that created them.

ADJUST YOUR RABBIT EARS

"We have two ears and one mouth so that we
might listen twice as much as we speak."
– Epictetus

If you've played golf for any length of time, you've likely heard someone remark that a certain player has "rabbit ears." Now, most of us who are old enough to remember the Nixon Administration have at least a faint recollection of the old rabbit ears sitting atop that black and white TV that looked more like a piece of furniture and likely bore the name Zenith, Sylvania, or RCA. It was the wire loop contraption you were constantly fiddling with in a vain attempt at pulling in better reception and cutting through the snow so you could watch shows long-since exiled to syndication like *Leave it to Beaver, Bewitched,* or *I Dream of Jeannie.*

When it comes to the game of golf, though, "rabbit ears" refers to a player who is in the habit of picking up every little unwanted noise and letting it distract them from playing the shot at hand and/or who blames each poor shot on some barely audible external factor. I used to play a lot of golf with a guy who never hit a bad shot that couldn't have been directly attributed to some rude individual two counties away that had honked their car horn during his downswing. Courtesy and proper etiquette are a fine thing, but if you are getting to the point where your playing partners are holding their breath for fear of being the responsible party when your ball goes careening into the woods (as it inevitably will), it might be time for some self-evaluation. Rabbit ears aren't something just reserved for amateurs, though, as even some of the best tour players can become afflicted with them. In the final round, on the final hole, when he was fifteen shots out of the lead, I once witnessed Gary Player back away from a bunker shot he had addressed because a lady on the walkway behind the grandstands some 75 yards away had laughed. When he skulled the shot after finally readdressing it, he glared back in the direction of the offending noise and raised his arms in disgust.

The funny thing about noise is it doesn't necessarily have to be viewed as a distraction or detrimental to what you are trying to accomplish. When it comes to focusing and your senses, you might be surprised to learn that you cannot truly f[

af

more than one of your senses at a time. Whether it

sound, taste, or smell, your brain's focus on any of

only singular in nature. In golf terms, this means that you cannot truly focus on the execution of your golf swing while you are at the same time listening intently to that lawnmower starting up nearby. Herein lies the perceived problem and the reason so many players blame their lack of execution on external distractions. I, however, want to be the first to tell you that this can actually be a good thing, especially if you are someone who tends to suffer from a lot of negative mental chatter as you stand over the ball. All you have to do is turn it around a bit.

Prior to initiating your golf swing, focus in on all the sounds taking place around you. On the driving range it might be the chatter of the fountain in the lake or a conversation taking place in the next stall over. On the course it could be a bird incessantly chirping in a nearby tree or a weekend warrior using his weed-whacker to eradicate months of backyard neglect. The sound isn't really important; your singular focus on that sound and nothing else is key. It is possible to initiate a swing while maintaining this focus, but instead of your usual swing, filled with all of the accompanying controlling swing instructions, mental chatter, and negative thoughts, you will be turning direction of the swing over to your subconscious mind. And for most of us, that is a good thing and can allow us to come as close as possible to making the most natural swing we have. So instead of chirping about how much all the offending nearby noises are ᴣcting your game, *adjust your rabbit ears* and try listening to them twice as much as before. If you do, there's a pretty good chance all those confounded cars driving by, cackling hens, and ill-timed conversations could actually end up being your proverbial ace in the hole.

SORRY BUD, OUR THREESOME'S FULL

*"I like long walks, especially when they're
taken by people who annoy me."*
– Noel Coward

Oh how we love to laud the game of golf for how it brings
out the best in people and encourages a brand of sportsmanship
that isn't exactly the hallmark of most other sports. The game,
however, can simultaneously serve as an arena for the ridiculous,
bringing out from time to time a less than flattering side of
people that they might not ordinarily display. Yes, it is true that
the game reveals character, but it often simultaneously exposes
us to some truly annoying, irritating, and obnoxious characters.

We've all played a time or two with someone whom we'd
rather not be subjected to a third. They're too slow, always

talking, always hawking (for balls, that is), too loud, the proverbial rules expert, bumping the ball, raking putts, or a litany of other things that can make their presence like nails on a chalkboard. The simple question, "Hey guys, got room for a fourth?" brings on a reflexive cringe or a sudden mood shift as you suddenly envision how your pleasant four-hour round is now gonna feel like six. The problem with this reaction is actually threefold. First of all, you were really anticipating a fun round, and it's a shame to let someone else ruin something that you otherwise were so looking forward to. Secondly, dealing with irritating and annoying people is just part of life, and by ducking that occasion, you are giving up an opportunity to practice and learn the patience and tolerance that life and golf so often demand. And finally, more often than most of us are willing to admit, that irritating guy in your foursome could be you.

There are numerous reasons why we find certain individuals so irritating, but one of the most common is because we are subconsciously attuned to certain characteristics that we would like to change about our own personalities. Being self-aware is one of the first and most important steps to making changes, along with recognizing the adjustments that we most likely need to make. So let's stop to take a look at some of the most irritating characters we find out there roaming the links and give you some clues on how to spot them in advance. And just in case you find you can't avoid them, when we're done, I promise to offer a little prescription that might have you looking forward the next round with Mr. or Ms. Obnoxious. Before we begin, though, I must warn you. While you will certainly recognize many of these characters and can possibly call some of them by name, hidden within the following descriptions is at least one character you won't instinctively find all that ridiculous but whose eerie familiarity might make you more than a bit uncomfortable.

<u>The Tortoise</u>. The Tortoise is a pack animal whose natural habitat is in the group just ahead of you. They're the ones never ready to hit when it's their turn, going back to the bag because they had the wrong club, flirting with the beverage cart girl, waiting for the green to clear for their second shot on that Par 5 (only to top it 10 feet once it finally does), and lining up their fourth putt from every conceivable angle. If you get paired with a Tortoise, a dead giveaway is their initial insistence of "Boy, I hate slow play!" while you're waiting around on the first tee, only to be followed by three practice swings, one back-off and restart of their entire pre-shot routine due to some offending nearby noise, and so many waggles you find yourself thinking, *Let's go, while we're young!*

<u>The Hare</u>. On the surface playing with a Hare might not seem like such a bad thing compared to the Tortoise, until he gets you into an altercation with the group in front of you for impatiently hitting into them ... for the third time! The Hare's need to "send a message" to the group up front also usually results in him yelling something like, "C'mon man, this isn't the PGA Tour!" while the group you're waiting on is putting out and

alternately looking at his watch every ten minutes like he's just about to miss a State Dinner. Hares rarely mark their ball or even putt out and will suggest something like, "You know if you don't put your club back in the bag after every shot and just wait to do it when you're selecting your club for the next shot, we could all save 15 minutes a round!"

The Ball-Hawker. This is the guy who's had the handle on his ball-retriever regripped more times than his clubs. The Ball-Hawker looks like a kid on an Easter egg hunt every time you approach a pond, barranca, or any other likely hiding spot for potential lost balls. He's never actually bought a golf ball from the pro shop and typically fires off with something like, "I can't believe you pay almost $5 apiece for those babies!" every time you open a new sleeve. The Ball-Hawker is typically recognized by the dirty towel hanging from his back pocket, traces of mud on his shoes and bottoms of his slacks, and his tendency to be found by the ball-washer on every tee polishing up a half-dozen or more of his most recent finds.

The Hollywood Handicapper. The Hollywood Handicapper loves to recount the time he went down to the wire in the club championship at some other club you've never heard of. He typically plays blades, uses Pro V1X (not the regular because he spins it too much), will show you how he just ground the sole on his wedges, and follows his inevitable topped tee shot on No. 1 with something like, "Rebuilding my swing right now. I expect that. Gonna take a little time to adjust." You can easily identify the Hollywood Handicapper by asking him what his handicap is. He will always begin his response by saying he used to be a scratch, a single digit, or at the very least something about 5-8 shots lower than he is right now, but injury, swing changes, a bad coach, a bad divorce, a bad case of vertigo, or some other excuse has caused him to "balloon" over the past year.

Golf Jargon Guy. You recognize Golf Jargon Guy by his uncanny ability to slip in just about every good, bad, and ugly golf saying during a round. He's got one ready for each and every situation and just can't seem to wait for you to leave a putt short so he can counter with, "Trip over your skirt, Alice?" or, "Never up, never in." Stuck in the woods? "Trees are 90 percent air," he says. He hits a drive down the middle, 50 yards farther than anything else he hit all day, and with understated humility replies, "That'll play." He knocks one into the next zip code to the right of the hole you're on and responds, "I've got a shot from there." "Stay up," "Sit," "Get legs," "Be the number," or "Run like you stole somethin'" will all be heard during a round with Golf Jargon Guy, along with the obligatory, "They don't draw pictures on the scorecard, boys," after the miraculous but inevitable recovery he makes at least once every time you play.

The Fanatic. Every club has at least one or two fanatics. They're the ones telling you about the sweet new Callaways they just saw last night on GolfWRX, mentioning how they had to hard-step the shafts on their new irons because they overwork the regular Dynamic Gold S-300s, always get their shafts pured, and typically want to talk the finer points of counter-weighting your grips because you know, "Ever since Nicklaus did it, that's been the real secret no one talks about." The Fanatic will only purchase clubs after going to The Institute or some other factory fitting site to try every conceivable combination currently available and will still have buyer's remorse, saying afterwards, "I probably should have waited for that new tour-issue shaft coming out from Aldila next month."

The Wannabe PGA Pro. The Wannabe PGA Pro can be spotted on the driving range or the practice putting green prior to your round. He'll approach you with a compliment, only to immediately follow it up with what you need to do. "You've got a pretty nice move. Beautiful tempo, too. You know if you just tweaked your grip a bit, closed that left foot a hair, and worked on your transition, you probably wouldn't fire the hips quite so early and you could get rid of that slice." He means well, but you didn't ask for the advice—and besides, your handicap is lower than his.

The Rules Official. Typically recognized by an up-to-date copy of the USGA Rulebook peeking from his back pocket. Instead of stopping you beforehand, he lies in wait for you to do something wrong and then says, "You know you could have taken a drop from there," in the most condescending manner. He is often witnessed interjecting in questionable situations (even those not in his own group) with something like, "Oh yeah, that's 24-2 Immovable Obstruction. You get your stance and one club length, not nearer the hole, no penalty." If you come across the Rules Official, be careful not to question his knowledge unless absolutely necessary, as he can become violently argumentative due to his reflexive need to be right, but when he finally and inevitably says, "I'll bet you a drink afterwards!" go ahead and do so because he, in fact, almost never is.

Mr. Mood Swing. Often seen in the golf shop asking to pick up the wedge he had re-shafted last week after it just mysteriously broke when he hit some (yet to be found) tree root right in the middle of the fairway on No. 7. Mr. Mood Swing is a club-thrower one minute and a fist-pumper the next. He will sulk for three holes after one bad one, curse wildly after a missed two-footer, and is invariably overheard telling himself, "You're horrible. Why don't you just give up the game if you're gonna play like such an idiot!" Only to follow it one shot later with, "Boo-yeah! That's what I'm talkin' about baby! That's what keeps you comin' back!"

Rico Suave. Every club has at least one or two of these peacocks. "It's better to look good than to play good" is their motto, and they live up to it with shoes, socks, gloves, caps, and even multi-colored belts that accessorize perfectly with every outfit. Rico generally prefers to go by the long form of his given name, such as Kenneth, Carlton, or James, rather than the simpler Ken, Carl, or Jim and will certainly be recognized by the almost runway-model-type strut he employs on the course and in and around the clubhouse. Rico is most often "fashionably late" to the tee due to his habit of trolling the sale rack in the golf shop and never strays far to look for a lost ball because, as he notes, "These are $300 all-Italian leather shoes. I'm certainly not ruining 'em for a $5 ball!"

Mr. Distracted. "Go ahead, guys. I'm right in the middle of a deal and I've got to get this one." If you are paired with Mr. Distracted, you can quickly recognize him by the fact that he is never really present. Constantly checking his cellphone for messages, the stock-ticker, the sports scores, and texting one person or another is the hallmark of Mr. Distracted. He will disappear suddenly to make a call that just can't wait and come back with, "Sorry, guys. Can you believe the line on the Bears/Packers over-under just moved to 42?" Mr. Distracted is also a particularly slow-playing partner on any scenic, historic, or ocean-side course due to his need to take a selfie with the Lone Cypress, the Swilcan Bridge, or any other golfing landmark in the background and then immediately text it to everyone he knows.

The Purist. The Purist is always fixing everyone else's divots and offering to give you a repair tool if you don't have one. Typically spotted refilling their sand bottles in the bucket on every par three, the purist can't understand why everyone else doesn't take better care of the course. Purists also love to decry any departure from the norm, can be heard poo-pooing long putters, or any other sort of non-conventional option, despite their own terrible case of the yips. Oftentimes you will spot a Purist walking the course or at least hear him touting the merits of walking and how it just gives you space to think and focus on your game. Around the bar you'll likely overhear him say something like, "Ever since we got away from persimmon, everything's gotten out of hand. They're taking the skill out of the game and making all the classic courses outdated. They should limit the flight of the ball!"

Mulligan Man. Mulligan Man loves his breakfast ball. "Didn't get time to warm up," he states flatly after teeing up a second ball on the first tee. "Hit until you're happy!" he continues with a wry smile. Mulligan Man can often be somewhat confused with the Hollywood Handicapper because his penchant for replaying shots throughout the round and not counting them also makes him one of the more self-delusional golfers out there, but Mulligan Man can be positively identified by the constant presence of a second ball in his right front pants pocket and a follow-through that has one hand reaching for it before the first ball has even landed.

The Stroke-Shaver. The first sign of the Stroke-Shaver is their almost irrational insistence on being the scorekeeper, but in the absence of that reality he will typically rattle off a confusing dramatization of his score like, "Let's see, one off the tee, two into the lake, hitting three, went in the bunker, two out, two putts—yeah, put me down for a six." The Stroke-Shaver also typically has the fastest golf cart and can be seen playing at least half a hole ahead of their own group, especially when their ball has headed towards any area that makes finding it in question; they will be heard shouting back to their playing partners something like, "Got it! Can't believe it stayed up—must've hit a tree or something."

The Hustler. The Hustler loves to gamble but always seems to be a bit short when it comes time to pay. "Oh shoot, you know I left my wallet in the truck. I thought it was in my bag. I'll get you next time," is one of his favorite standbys. He seems to live by Trevino's famous line, "You don't know pressure until you play for five bucks with only two in your pocket," has been accused of being in on more than one *parking lot split*, and will almost certainly insist on going double-or-nothing on the last hole once he's lost the bet. If you want to avoid a confrontation, just move along to another group as soon as you hear anything like, "We're playing automatic two-down presses, right?"

The Big Brag. The braggart of the group is always telling you about the golf trip they were just on in Bandon Dunes, Pebble Beach, or St. Andrews. They love to recount the story about how their buddy got 'em on Cypress that time and they ended up playing with a tour player. He name-drops incessantly about the invitational he played in at some ritzy private club, the celebrity he's tight with after being paired together that one time in a Pro-Am, or how he was invited to play Augusta and had to turn it down due to a work conflict. A dead giveaway is how he starts every story with something like, "Reminds me of that time I was playing..."

Now there are definitely some characters that I've missed, but I think you get the point. Truth be told, at least if we're willing to admit it, we can all likely find at least a little bit of ourselves in many of the descriptions, and by learning to laugh a little bit at our own quirks along the way, we will go a long way to learning the patience to tolerate the foibles and idiosyncrasies that everyone displays from time to time. But since I promised more than just perspective, I will now offer up an actual method for dealing with Mr. or Ms. Obnoxious the next time you're subjected to them, just in case your newfound self-awareness isn't quite enough to get you all the way through that next round. What should you do? Well, here is what I'm suggesting. Fight fire with fire and confront the ridiculous with something even more ridiculous. You might run the risk of annoying those who annoy you, but the next time it happens, I want you to use libation to mitigate the irritation.

What? Did I just suggest drinking as a solution to dealing with irritating characters on the golf course or elsewhere in life? Well, not necessarily, but I am suggesting a form of the age-old college drinking game to help turn the ridiculous into the sublime the next time you're out there. You don't actually have to drink alcohol to play this game, and for that matter, you don't even really have to drink. What you want to do (either by yourself or in cahoots with a fellow playing partner or two who shares your feelings about Mr. or Ms. Obnoxious) is stipulate prior to the next round a particular phrase or action that is a hallmark of their irritation and agree to drink, chuckle, or even just nod or wink every time they roll out the ol', "I'd rather be lucky than good!"

Now I definitely don't want to encourage irresponsibility to counter irritation, so if you do prefer to play the alcoholic version on this game, please make sure to arrange for rides home after the round. If your Mr. or Ms. Obnoxious is a strong enough offender to merit playing in the first place, then it will definitely be the responsible course of action. But it doesn't take alcohol to enjoy the game and find a little humor in what has heretofore been something that drove you crazy. It's just a matter of perspective. Sure you could play the confrontation game and call that other person out for being so obnoxious, but in the end how fun would that really be? And don't forget the value in learning a little patience and tolerance, since you never really know—in someone else's eyes, that irritating person might just be you. So the next time you hit a bad shot and instinctively reach for that second ball and dejectedly say, "Right in the lumberyard!" or slam your club back in your bag in frustration, step back a moment and take a look at your partners. Did they just reach for their drinks? If so, maybe it's time you learn to work on toning down your own brand of golf course antics. Or the next time you walk up to the guys in the clubhouse and ask, "Hey guys, got room for a fourth?" you might just hear, "Sorry bud, our threesome's full."

PART 3

ON INSECURITY,

ANXIETY, AND

NEGATIVITY

REJECT THE ILLUSION OF SECURITY

"Security is mostly a superstition. It does not
exist in nature, nor do the children of men as
a whole experience it. Avoiding danger is no
safer in the long run than outright exposure.
Life is either a daring adventure or nothing!"
– Helen Keller

In golf, as in life, we often find that our most
consequential decisions come at times when the stakes are
highest. In golf it is at times like these that we are free to be a
more daring swashbuckling type of player who trades high risk
for the promise of high reward ... or he who would chose the
safer, more secure path, one that mitigates the downside threat to
his score and ego in trade for completely foregoing the upside
promise of salvation and the shot of adrenaline and increased

self-confidence that comes from pulling off a heroic shot. Curiously, in the generally accepted lexicon of the game, the safer, more conservative route is often referred to as the smart play, while the riskier play is often labeled as dumb, even when it comes off. But is it really so totally cut and dry? Would Bubba Watson have won his first Masters if he had played smart and just punched out to the fairway on hole No. 10 during the playoff in 2012? Likely not. And even if he had, he would certainly not now be known for having hit one of the greatest shots in Major Championship history. Benjamin Franklin once said, "Those who would sacrifice freedom for safety deserve neither." Whether or not Franklin was among the early practitioners of the game is a matter of some debate, but if he was, one could imagine him declaring that in the clubhouse bar after a round at St. Andrews (the university there awarded him an honorary degree)—a round in which he had lost an event by one shot after succumbing to the siren's song of security and the illusion that the safe play is always both the smarter play and the surest path to better scores and victory.

As human beings we inherently crave security. Our brains are hard-wired to seek it as a response to threats that are both real and imagined. Evaluating and consequently reacting to these threats is the job of one of the most primitive parts of our brains: the amygdala. This region of our brain processes base emotions resulting from sensory inputs like fear, insecurity, and anxiety. It's one of the oldest and least evolved regions of the brain and is responsible for the rush of adrenaline and other hormones injected into your bloodstream (as well as the elevated heart rate, increased muscle tension, and sweaty palms) you get every time you see, hear, or feel something that you assess as a potential danger. We have a second line of defense that is unique to mammals and that has evolved more recently known as the neo-cortex. It is a more advanced part of the brain that is both intelligent and analytic. It can both reason and assess the nature of threats and is more nuanced than the amygdala. There is but one problem: it is just a bit slower.

So this brings us to a bit of a conundrum. We have two regions of our brain wrestling to control our reactions to threats and risks to our security, and they are mostly operating in parallel, rather than in conjunction. The more advanced and analytic neo-cortex struggles to win this battle with our more primitive amygdala because it is relatively slow afoot; consequently, you find us reacting to perceived threats and risks to our security almost as if we are helpless to do otherwise. Fortunately, in the game of golf, the threats we face are for the most part not anywhere near life or death—but try telling that to your primitive amygdala. It reacts to the prospect of embarrassing yourself by topping it off the first tee in front of your buddies and a small gathering of unknown onlookers much in the same way early homo sapiens did when a saber-toothed tiger jumped out of the bushes while he was out collecting wood for that night's fire. This reaction is a brilliantly designed mechanism for immediately fleeing for one's life, but the added adrenaline and cortisol pumped into your system at these times isn't much use when it comes to trying to keep your tee shots on the short stuff or your ball out of the lake that fronts that tricky par three.

Fortunately for us, our brains managed to learn a new trick just a short few million years ago, and we can now appropriately predict the timing, location, and severity of many threats before they materialize based upon our past experiences. This new trick allows us to make the aforementioned trade-offs, and in golf, one of the ways we do this is by trading the freedom of that free-wheeling, free-swinging move we make with the driver under normal circumstances for that iron off the tee on a short and tight par four. On another hole, we do it by laying up short of the water, when we fear that trying to reach the green is a somewhat risky proposition based upon the length of the carry, the ball's lie, and our past experiences. The neo-cortex is essentially the region of the brain that has the biggest influence upon whether a particular course of play is perceived as either smart or dumb. And while this new and still-evolving region of the brain allows us the opportunity to plan ahead and make these sorts of decisions, it has its own hang-ups. When you combine its ability to anticipate perceived threats along with the amygdala's penchant for exaggerating the degree of their risk to your security, you often end up with a desire to seek the comfort of the "smart" course of action, and this illusion of security can seem too powerful to overcome. If you really think about it, though, and you turn those decisions completely over to your newer neo-cortex, you just might find you won't always end up making those same seemingly safe and smart decisions.

So now that you have a basic understanding of your brain (at least these two particular areas of it and how they can affect your game), you can learn to teach one perspective while using the advantages of the other. And one of the advantages of having this newly evolved neo-cortex is that we can envision situations and scenarios that have caused us to overreact in the past and decide what the appropriate course of action should have been. And once we have done that, we will have begun the process of changing our mental programs so that the associated risks and threats are no longer actually perceived as threats or at least their threat level is kept in perspective. This is a process, and while it doesn't necessarily happen overnight, with conscious intention and discipline, I promise it won't take as long as the primitive homo sapien had to wait for a fledgling neo-cortex to come along and aid in counteracting his amygdala. So the next time you're in a tournament (or even a casual round with your buddies) and you reach a hole or a situation that typically causes you to reflexively trade a little bit of freedom for what you think will keep you safe, *reject the illusion of security*, because in the immortal words of Helen Keller, it might just be time to go live your daring adventure.

AVOID AVOIDANCE

"When fear makes your choices for you, no security measures on earth will keep the things you dread from finding you. But if you can avoid avoidance, if you can choose to embrace experiences out of passion, enthusiasm, and a readiness for feeling whatever arises, then nothing, nothing in all this dangerous world can keep you from being safe."
– Martha Beck

In the medical dictionary, *avoidance behavior* is described as a conscious or unconscious defense mechanism by which a person tries to escape from unpleasant situations or feelings, such as nervousness, anxiety, and fear. While on the surface this might seem a bit of an odd topic to introduce to a discussion of golf, it is a concept that is all too familiar to those who play, whether they realize it or not. In analyzing this behavior, it is striking how similar its causes and the situations in which it manifests itself are, regardless of the level of player. It can be the player who lacks confidence in shots under 100 yards who consistently lays up to distances that will leave him nothing less than a full swing. In other instances we see it in players who consistently miss the ball wildly in one particular direction due to a fear of missing it in the opposite way. A third common manifestation is the player who dreads those two-foot putts who is consistently trying to lag even fairly short putts, due to their desire to avoid leaving themselves with another one of those knee-knocking come-backers. Or finally it is the all-too-common problem we see with players who refuse to engage in competition altogether, due to insecurities about their game or their swing not quite being up to the level of where they think it should be to compete.

Now any armchair psychologist can tell you the problem with avoidance behavior is that the more you avoid something, the bigger place it begins to occupy in your mind and the more difficult it is to get over. The more often we avoid it and the longer we avoid it, the more difficult it becomes to confront when we finally attempt to do so, as it seems to magically take on a life of its own. Every athlete feels nervousness; it is what he or she decides to do with that nervous energy that makes each of them different. If they become afraid of those feelings and allow them to change how they compete, it is a sign that they have developed a problem.

In the attempt to identify those most likely to adopt avoidance behavior and why, there are innumerable studies and theories to go around. Many claim that those with personality traits associated with low achievement motivation (the stereotype in some cases for Type B's) will also experience the greatest anxiety in pressure situations. And when those same Type B personalities feel their performance is being evaluated, they are most likely to do what they can to avoid those types of situations. There is also a lot of credence to the arguments that claim this type of behavior often stems from an ego-centric mindset that places far too great a value on the prospect of looking good (or at least not looking bad) in any given situation. Establishing the root of the problem through some sort of Freudian-type investigation of your past or analysis of your psyche, however, is not nearly as important as is the simple recognition of any of these tendencies and a desire to find out how to change them.

This essentially brings us back to the idea of what avoidance behavior is: a defense mechanism against the uncomfortable feelings of nervousness, anxiety, or fear. Scientist Walter Bradford Cannon first coined the term *fight-or-flight response*, that instinct towards hyper-arousal we display during threatening situations (you might remember) that is left over from our caveman days. It was very useful when we were trying to escape from that aforementioned saber-toothed tiger and for helping our brains to remember how best to avoid those dangerous situations, but it isn't very useful when it comes to playing competitive golf. Every situation in life is essentially what we perceive it to be, so is it possible that the root of the problem lies in our perception of these threats and the consequences of success or failure in a given situation? Whose opinion is so important that we are afraid of looking like less of a golfer or hoping to appear as more of one in front of them? What amount of success or failure could really and truly change our lives? And how could anything related to the game of golf have become so distorted in our minds that we could come to perceive the negative consequences of any related failure to be an actual threat?

I mentioned in the previous chapter that Helen Keller once said, "Life is either a daring adventure or nothing!" Now, I don't necessarily want to compare the obstacles that she overcame to those that we face in our golf games, but a lot can be learned from someone whose mindset and whose perspective towards the obstacles life presented her was so obviously positive and who lacked anything remotely resembling timidity. What do we really have to lose? Far less than what we have to gain. So if you find yourself in or approaching situations where your insecurities instinctively make you anxious, the most important thing you need to do is *avoid avoidance* and embrace those experiences with passion and enthusiasm. If we meet those challenges head on, again and again and again, our continued exposure will allow us to learn how we can change our responses to them. And just how do you develop the courage to do that? Start with changing your perception of these situations by coming to terms with what the true consequences of success or failure in them ultimately means. And once you're able to do that, you will begin to develop an ability to handle almost anything in life that arises, as well as the sense of peace that comes from knowing that nothing at all can ever really keep you from feeling truly safe.

WAIT 'EM OOT

"Come back to where'er ye were a minute ago.

Wait 'em oot."

– Shivas Irons, *Golf in the Kingdom*

When it comes to dealing with the anxiety created by unwanted thoughts on the golf course, a passage from one of my favorite golf books, *Golf in the Kingdom* by Michael Murphy, invariably comes to mind. Murphy, the protagonist in the story, following an awful front nine with his newfound mentor, the mysterious Scottish teaching pro Shivas Irons, unexpectedly turns it around by starting the back nine with a pair of pars, lifting his spirits a bit before coming to the twelfth at Burningbush...

...I could only sustain it for a while. On the twelfth hole our drive was into the wind, down a narrow fairway that dog-legged to the right. Familiar images of disaster came back to haunt me as I took my stance. I sliced the drive and the sea breeze carried it into the rough. Shivas walked alongside me up the fairway and asked me what I was thinking. I told him about the awful thoughts. "They'll pass," Shivas said, "if ye daena' fight them. Come back to where'er ye were a minute ago. Wait 'em oot."

I'm not sure wiser words have ever been uttered by any teaching pro, real or imagined. I first read them close to twenty years ago, but it is only in the past few years that I have come to really appreciate their wisdom.

The majority of us who've played for any length of time have certainly been faced with a similar situation. We step up to the ball after having gone through our normal routine with nothing seemingly unordinary going on in our heads or in the game when it occurs. At other times, it might happen during an important tournament or event, while stepping up to the first tee, or when playing with someone we desperately hope to impress. Visions of wild shots careening to the left and right, into hazards, into the woods, or out of bounds suddenly invade our consciousness. The fairway that looked wide and inviting only moments before seems a mere hallway lined with trees whose gnarled branches reach out like aged hands to snag even the most slightly offline drive. Bunkers look like vast beaches and water hazards as expansive as oceans, with the distant target as small and obscure as a speck on the horizon. You experience tightness in your chest, your breathing gets shallow (if you breathe at all), and a suffocating sense, not dissimilar to claustrophobia, creeps over you. These strong images and subsequent feelings of anxiety inexplicably invade your mind and very quickly take on a life all their own.

Now for some this may sound like an exaggeration, but I promise the rest of you, you've got far more than Mr. Murphy to keep you company. We all deal with unwanted and unproductive thoughts from time to time on the golf course. Even the best tour players occasionally have them (and oftentimes at the most critical moments), but whether you're a tour player or a weekend warrior, they can be frustrating, bewildering, and destructive, if you let them. Where do these thoughts come from? Why do they come in what seems like an instant and at the most inopportune times? What can you do about them, and how do you make them go away?

Everyone has millions of random thoughts throughout each and every day, and for most of these, you have learned to just recognize them for what they are without acting on them. For some reason, however, when we step over a golf ball, we seem to reflexively take these thoughts more seriously and almost unwittingly respond to the apparent threat they present to our games. A useful practice for dealing with these unproductive waves of thought comes from our friends the Buddhists. It is a valuable exercise for golfers in that it teaches us not to fight these waves of thought, but rather just to roll with them. You ride them up and down like an offshore buoy and let them run their course, as they eventually will, rather than emphatically attempting to banish them to some space in the nether-regions of your mind.

So in a nutshell, the fastest way to get rid of unwanted negative thoughts is not to try to get rid of them. Don't struggle with your thoughts; just recognize them for what they are: thoughts. And if you don't assign too much importance or emotion to any one of them, they will make you less and less anxious each time as you come to accept their impermanence. So the next time you're on the first tee and images of "awful things" come to mind, don't panic or descend into full-blown anaphylactic shock. I understand it may seem a bit difficult at first, especially from where you stand at the moment, but just remember the immortal words of Shivas because "they'll pass" if you just *"wait 'em oot."* And so while it took nigh on two decades for me to appreciate those pearls of wisdom, I hope that for many of you they will hit home the first time.

TAKE A DEEP BREATH

"Anxiety is a deep conscious breath
away from dissolving."
– Mike Dolan

I was reading a book the other day in which the author commented that common sense doesn't necessarily equate to common action. The truth of that statement really struck me at the time. There are so many times in life that we either can do or should do something that would be beneficial to us, but we choose not to for one reason or another. We know that eating that whole large pepperoni pizza followed by a pint of Ben & Jerry's adds a little extra tread to that spare around our midsection, yet we often do it anyway and justify it because at least we washed it down with a two-liter bottle of *diet* soda. We know that exercise is good for us, relieves stress, helps aid weight loss, and has a host of other health benefits, yet somehow we can never seem to find the time due to the never-ending list of eminently more important things we absolutely must do (like that hourly Facebook status update). Keeping this in mind, I guess it's no small wonder that while some estimates claim up to 90 percent of Americans are chronically dehydrated, causing all sorts of problems for us, water remains about as close to free as any consumable we have access to and is never likely more than 30 steps away from us at any given moment.

And since golf mirrors life, it isn't surprising that at least part of the answer to many of our struggles in the game are literally right in front of our faces, too. Just as in our eternal quest for weight loss and health, we are too often ignoring things that are just common sense while we search for more complicated or cryptic solutions. It is that never-ending quest for a magic bullet, miracle cure, or easier path that very often leads us astray and away from some of the simpler answers available to us. When it comes to golf and many of our struggles with learning to relax and get comfortable on the course, one such answer is breathing.

I work with a number of students who play a lot of competitive golf, and one of the things I often have to remind them to do is breathe, especially when they find themselves in pressure situations. Breathing is something we do unconsciously most of the time, so to have to remind someone to do it may sound borderline ridiculous, but that is precisely the reason it is necessary to remind people to do it. We put the process of breathing on autopilot so much so that we don't really analyze how we do it, when we start and stop doing it, how often we do it, and why. The process of breathing, how we do it, and how often we do it has a whole host of effects upon our physical body and mental state. Slowing down your breathing and breathing more deeply has a great deal of positive benefits from decreasing muscle tension, reducing stress and anxiety, and helping to increase focus and concentration. When we are nervous and stressed, our breathing gets very shallow and short, verging on hyperventilation. This is another one of those leftover reactions from our caveman days when stress and anxiety was often the precursor to the triggering of the aforementioned *fight-or-flight response*, helping to supply us with extra adrenaline and oxygen to our awaiting muscles. Back then this was absolutely essential in our quest to avoid all sorts of life-threatening predators. Fast-forward to today, however, and the tension in our muscles and hyper-alertness brought on by this condition isn't typically very useful when it comes to the game of golf. We need to learn to increase our variable heart rate in order to relax during pressure situations, and one of the best ways to do that is to control our breathing. Here is a little trick.

Take a few quiet moments at home in a place where you won't be interrupted. Breathe in and out as normally as possible and count how many breaths you take in one minute, with both the inhale and the exhale counting as one breath. Now if you are like most of my students, if I asked you how many breaths per minute you typically take, you would have no idea and likely have never even thought about it. If you aren't stressed (or terribly overweight) and are in a normal relaxed state, you will likely find that you take somewhere between 12 and 20 breaths per minute. That means each breath takes you roughly three to five seconds. When you are nervous and stressed, however, that number can often rise to well above 20, and along with it, so do your feelings of nervousness, your inability to focus, and increased tension in your muscles.

To combat this, learn to count your breaths in between shots and make taking at least a couple of deep belly breaths part of your pre-shot routine. Studies show that if you can lower your breathing to under 12 breaths a minute, you will significantly decrease your feelings of stress, anxiety, and muscle tension, while increasing your ability to focus. This equates to taking each inhale and exhale roughly to a count of three. And while this common action sounds on the surface like it is only common sense, it is amazing how our natural human instincts override this most basic of actions. So the next time you're headed to the first tee, are facing that long carry shot over water, or are staring down that knee-knocking three-footer for all the marbles, don't forget to *take a deep breath*. It may not make it automatic, but it will automatically make you more relaxed and much more able to focus on the task at hand.

MAKE MEANINGFUL MISTAKES

"If you're not making mistakes, you're not doing anything. I'm positive a doer makes mistakes."
– John Wooden

When it comes to golf and much of everything else that we do in life, we all see our experiences through a different-colored lens that has been crafted by our past experiences and our chosen interpretation of them. While the nature of our internal conversations can be very complex, for simplicity's sake let's just say that most of us likely fall into two basic categories: optimists and pessimists. How we play, enjoy, and progress in our games can often be directly attributed to whether or not we view our experiences through the "rose-colored" lens of the optimist or through the sort of dingy sepia tones of the Murphy's Law-type pessimist. While neither of these perspectives is technically the truth, one leaves the door open to progress while the other impedes it, and one will leave you enjoying the game much more, regardless of your level of play.

One of the more famous doers in history was Thomas Edison, and when asked about his struggles early in the invention of the electric light bulb, Edison, in response to his critics, said, "I have not failed 700 times. I have not failed even once. I have succeeded in proving that those 700 ways will not work. When I have eliminated all the ways that will not work, I will find the way that will." Can you see the possibilities in this type of thinking? Can you imagine how beneficial this sort of perspective would be to anyone who wished to accomplish anything? Well, the good news is that we have a choice in how we decide to perceive things, and with a little introspection, we can begin to change if we find our way of thinking is less than constructive.

Here is a little exercise to begin the process. Pay attention to the mistakes you make during your next round of golf. What does the little voice in your head tell you after each one? For some, that voice is so strong, it might actually escape the confines of their heads and blurt out something like, "Idiot!" "Choke-artist!" "You're terrible!" ... or even things much worse. If you find yourself saying or thinking these types of things after a mistake, then challenge yourself to change not only the nature of your internal conversation, but also what you do during those moments. This is not just simply eliminating negative self-talk, which is in and of itself a useful exercise, but actually replacing that talk with a new type of conversation that is more productive and a period of reflection that gives you the space to do so. Here is what it might look like.

If you hit an anxious snap-hook into the woods on hole No. 1 with a bunch of people watching, take a brief moment and think back to what led to it. Did you get out of your routine? Did you maintain a relaxed grip pressure? Were you picturing where you didn't want the ball to go, rather than your target at the last instant? It doesn't really matter what the mistake was, but rather that you make a habit of spending a moment reflecting upon the small space of time just prior to the mistake in a way that you can learn from it. Finally, finish the process by affirming the mistake with a positive closing statement that cements your commitment to change. In your head it might sound like this: "O.K., I guess that's what happens when I allow nervousness to rush my pre-shot routine. Next time I will slow down, remember to take a deep breath after the practice swing, and keep an image of the target in my mind's eye after my last look until I send the ball on its way." When you focus on something, it grows, so if you want your game to grow, make sure that you're focusing on and interpreting your experiences in an "Edisonian" way. You will be taking advantage of the opportunity to learn from every experience. Do that, and from now on, you will not just make mistakes, you'll *make meaningful mistakes.*

SLICE IT INTO THE WOODS!

"It so amazes you how much stage fright you get. I've been in front of cameras all my life, but that first tee, standing over that ball that's not even moving, it's scarier than doing a movie!"
– Michael Douglas

I've always thought it curious that when actors or musicians get ready to head out for a big performance, people say, "Break a leg!" The origins of this saying are a bit obscure, but the generally accepted explanation is that superstitious performers historically felt that wishing someone good luck right before a performance was actually bad luck, so at some point they began to do the opposite to help cut the tension and drive away stage fright. When it comes to competitive golf, I suppose this would be something akin to saying, "Chunk it in the lake!" or, "Hook it out of bounds!" to a player on the first tee just prior to them teeing off in the U.S. Open.

Now as superstitious as golfers are, I suppose it's not all that curious to find that this reverse psychology sort of approach has failed to find any sort of foothold in the game to date. In the game of golf, it would be considered, at the least, very bad form to mention a potential hazard prior to a fellow competitor playing a shot, and at the worst, it would be seen as downright gamesmanship. This fear of planting a negative mental seed in a golfer's mind is so prevalent and generally accepted that many golfers are afraid to even say or hear the word *shank* for fear of it somehow mystically spreading like some sort of viral disease. So why, as golfers, are we so petrified of negative mental imagery? Well there are some very scientific answers to this mystical phenomenon, but as is so often the case with mysterious occurrences, explanations that one might categorize as fantastical or far-fetched seem to be the ones that are most readily accepted.

Golf and mysticism have been entwined as long as the game has been chronicled, and the predominant influence of the mental side of the game was a subject of discussion in even the earliest writings on the game. Arnold Haultain wrote a book called *The Mystery of Golf* in 1908, long before the authors of more famous tomes like *Golf in the Kingdom*, *Zen Golf*, or *The Legend of Bagger Vance* were even born, and it discussed many of the game's mysteries and dilemmas in ways that sound nearly as current as if they were part of the post-round discussion in the press tent after one of today's PGA Tour events. In these books and many others, a common thread can be found in the discussion of the effects of both positive and negative imagery on one's golf game. And while across the generations it has been generally accepted that positive imagery is as much a benefit to one's game as negative is bad, it is the discussion of the application of positive visualization techniques, the implementation of methods to avert negative imagery, and the processes with which to balance the two that can often range from the sublime to the ridiculous to the borderline supernatural.

And truth be told, I often find these more romanticized, mystical, and less than scientific discussions of the subject to be not only more entertaining, but often somehow more engaging than some of the more recent scientific studies that back them up. Now, trying to distill them all down to one method or process would not only rob you of the opportunity to read some of the best golf literature ever written, but it would also be an injustice to the tremendous variety of great information that is out there. What works for one is often different than what does for another. That being said, however, I will say that, in at least some situations, it might not be a bad idea to take a cue from our nearly equally superstitious cousins in the performing arts and address them head on. As I've already mentioned, thoughts are just thoughts. Assigning too much significance to any one thought or recurring thought gives it far too much weight and significance in the mind and can allow it to develop into an actual thing we would fear. This is very often how phobias and mental blocks begin. The process of recognizing these thoughts for what they are and accepting them can help to trivialize them and reduce their significance. And while I'm not suggesting most golfers are ready for you to pull an Al Czervik and bet them 100 bucks they'll "slice it into the woods!", I am suggesting that you might try adopting a more irreverent approach and tell yourself that (or something similar) the next time you face a shot that makes you particularly anxious. At best, it just might be a different enough approach that it helps you relax and execute your intention. And at the worst? Well there's always the foot wedge and, uh, yes, winter rules!

PART 4

ON DISCIPLINE,

HABITS, AND ROUTINES

THE BEST LAID SCHEMES

"In reading the lives of great men, I found that the first victory they won was over themselves. Self-discipline with all of them came first."
– Harry S. Truman

What seems like a lifetime ago, I remember whiling away many a late-summer afternoon with a few other hotshot young players at the local club putting for a buck or two when we were bored. One such afternoon, when it was just myself and one other buddy, we were interrupted unexpectedly when the grizzled old club professional stepped out of the pro shop and walked over to us.

"What are you guys gonna do with yourselves?" he said.

"What???" we replied almost in unison, not really sure what he meant.

"What are you going to do with yourselves?" he repeated. "With your lives. You're wasting your time out here. You can't spend the rest of your lives putting for pennies."

"We're gonna play on tour," I said matter-of-factly, as if it was a foregone conclusion.

And without hesitation my buddy chimed in, "Yeah we're getting ready for the tour. This is homework."

"Hah! You guys aren't gonna play no tour!" he fired back with mocking laughter, all at once calling us out and throwing a huge bucket of ice water on our bravado. "You don't have the discipline. If any of you really wanted to play the tour, you'd be out here every morning before school playing nine holes or practicing. There isn't a one of you out here that has the kind of self-discipline it takes to make it on tour!"

Having said his piece, he turned and walked back inside, chuckling to himself and seemingly satisfied with not only having put us young whippersnappers in our place, but at the same time having thrown down the proverbial gauntlet. Well, as anyone who's ever told a teenager they can't do something will likely tell you, it worked, at least for a little while, as on the spot my buddy and I agreed to meet at the course every morning at 5:00 A.M. prior to school. We would tee off in the dark, carrying flashlights to help find our balls and enough confidence in our ability that we could essentially play the first couple of holes blind until the day broke. That old pro had taught both of us a handful of lessons about golf and life, but to this day I don't really know whether or not he intended that to be one of those coaching moments. By calling us out like he did, though, he ended up teaching both of us one of our first real lessons in self-discipline and the art of making a plan to accomplish something.

Despite that early lesson, I obviously never made it on tour, but almost thirty years later, I still have lofty ambitions. If I am guilty of one thing for sure, it is habitually planning to accomplish more than the hours in a day will allow. And while my habit of over-planning can leave me at times frustrated when things like, oh, the necessity to actually sleep from time to time get in the way, I am simultaneously grateful for it, because it has forced me to continually learn valuable lessons in self-discipline, lest I be resigned to forever underachieving. One of the things that I learned from getting up before daybreak every day for a couple of months to play golf (until frost and an angry superintendent finally chased us off for the season) was essentially that self-discipline is developing the habit of making and keeping commitments to yourself. The other thing it brought into focus for me was that if you have a goal, you need to have a plan for accomplishing it.

The French writer Antoine de Saint-Exupery said, "A goal without a plan is just a wish." For most of us, golf is a passion and a labor of love, and while there are few of us with as lofty goals as that buddy of mine and I had that summer, we all likely have a least some unspoken goals for our golf game. And while even the best laid plans cannot always predict where we will end up, it is necessary to learn the art of self-discipline if we wish to carry out any plan. Maybe you're tired of three-putting and you believe being a better putter will help you finally get your handicap down into single digits. Well, you can use that goal to develop a plan that will help you start the process of learning self-discipline.

The first thing you need to do is schedule a couple of daily tasks related to your goal. If you can't make it to the course first thing every morning, buy a putting cup or some similar contraption you can use at home. For a period of two months, get up every morning 15 minutes earlier and spend that time practicing your putting. Then schedule another time every day where you will do the exact same thing. It could be sneaking over to the course on your lunch hour, dropping by the club on your way home from the office, or putting to your practice cup again 15 minutes prior to bed at night. The important thing is to schedule it at exactly the same time each day and stick to that time for the stated period. Avoid acting on impulse and saying to yourself you'll do it at a different time one day because you feel like hitting the snooze button one more time or a colleague asks you to lunch. It's an appointment you have with yourself, and keeping that appointment is more important than whether or not the exercise ultimately improves your putting. Track your progress, and at the end of the allotted time, take a look at how you did, where you might have slipped up, and if so why.

Now as far as my own golf game goes, fortunately my current plan doesn't involve paying my mortgage with the proceeds from any tournament winnings that I expect to be coming my way anytime soon. The busyness of the golf season and the myriad of responsibilities related to that, combined with the full slate of activities us parents of young children are invariably involved in and the desire to complete this book, have all conspired to put my own game on somewhat of a sabbatical. I arise each morning at 5:00 A.M., 90 minutes earlier than I really need to most days, so I can spend some quiet time writing before I help get my daughters up and take them to school. If we really stop to think about it, we all have times in our life where we find ourselves in places and situations that aren't exactly where we originally envisioned we'd be. And we all have known times when meeting our responsibilities requires that some of our passions (like playing golf) must be put on the back burner for just a while. In my own situation, I am grateful for that and for the lessons it has taught me, and I truly wouldn't want it any other way.

So as I've already mentioned, I am an avid collector of quotes, and as my staff would confirm for you, I like to end each meeting with a famous one that is topical and that I feel will make them think. This little story and the topics of planning and self-discipline for me bring to mind one of history's most commonly cited quotations, one that I believe fairly often sums up how we all feel about the subjects. It comes from the poem *To a Mouse*, written by Scottish national poet Robert Burns in 1785. While most of us today are familiar with a more distilled version of it, the original reads, "The best laid schemes o' Mice an' Men,

Gang aft agley, An' lea'e us nought but grief an' pain, for promis'd joy!"

Scotland, it is often said, has given the world three great gifts: Burns, whiskey, and golf. And while history seems to have forgotten whether or not Burns was indeed a golfer, his poetry and famous ballads like "Auld Lang Syne" suggest more than a passing familiarity with whiskey at least. Given that, his birthplace, and the insightful wisdom he possessed for one who died so young (age 37), one can only imagine he must have whiled away at least a few of his summer afternoons on the links playing his country's national pastime or partaking in some post-round revelry in the clubhouses of historic places like Prestwick, Carnoustie, or St. Andrews, putting off at least for just a moment his own best laid plans.

PERFECT THE ART OF PERFECT PRACTICE

*"Practice does not make perfect. Only
perfect practice makes perfect."*
– Vince Lombardi

When it comes to elite-level performance in nearly every endeavor, from music to football to golf, it has long been conventional wisdom that the majority of those people that we admire and whose performances we dream to emulate are born with a special gift for doing what they do. From Mozart to Jerry Rice to Tiger Woods, there is a prevailing notion that these individuals (or anyone else who excels at an extremely high level in their chosen field) were born with a gift, a superior level of talent that enables them to perfect their craft at levels beyond that of ordinary men.

Author Geoff Colvin, in his book *Talent is Overrated*, argues to the contrary. Upon closer inspection, he says you most often find that a primary factor that separates the good from the great is the way in which they practice their chosen craft and the volume of such practice they undertake. An impressive amount of research has been done over the past few decades in relation to elite performance and the factors that determine why some succeed at such high levels over others. In nearly every case, the unifying element among those who succeed at the top level of their craft is extensive deliberate practice, often as much as **10,000** hours or more, with a singular focus on the specific areas an individual would like to improve upon. Let's look briefly at some examples Colvin and others have used for evidence to back this up.

Wolfgang Amadeus Mozart has long been widely considered the ultimate example of the "divinely gifted" theory of greatness. He supposedly composed music at the tender age of five, gave public performances as a pianist at age eight, and went on to produce hundreds of works that are widely regarded as treasures of western culture, all in the brief time before his death at age 35. If you look a little deeper, though, you would learn that Mozart's father, Leopold Mozart, was a domineering parent and expert music teacher who began Mozart on a program of intensive training at age three. Further investigation has brought to light the fact that, in truth, the majority of his early compositions were likely written mostly by his father and were really little more than compilations from works of other composers, containing no original music. These early works are now regarded as insignificant and the work of a typical student who had been training since a very early age. His first masterpiece, the Piano Concerto No. 9, wasn't actually written until the age of 21, and his apparent ability to compose entire works in his head came from a letter that he supposedly wrote which has since been declared a forgery. Close examination of all his existing manuscripts reveal that his method of composition was actually a painstaking practice of continual trial and revision that took years, a method not significantly different from that of most of his contemporaries. As it turns out, Mozart practiced hard to perfect his craft, and during his lifetime, the fruits of his labor were actually fairly ordinary.

Jerry Rice, one of the most prolific receivers in the history of football, had to be persuaded to try out for his high school team, and even though he was a standout player, only one small college, Mississippi Valley State, offered him a scholarship. Again a standout in college, he was drafted in the NFL but was passed over by 15 teams before being picked by the 49ers because his speed was barely average by NFL standards. So what ended up making him the greatest receiver in history? His dedication to practice. During the season, Rice arrived early and left after everyone else each day, and he had six-day-a-week off-season strength and conditioning workouts that were notorious throughout the league. Other players would occasionally join Rice during his practice regimen, and many often got sick trying to keep up with him. He also spent an incredible amount of time with coaches, reviewing game film, and studying playbooks. Upon further analysis of his career, it has been revealed that Rice spent only 1 percent of his time actually playing football. The other 99 percent was spent deliberately practicing the things that would help insure his success during the games.

Tiger Woods, who earlier in his career was often referred to as "the Mozart of golf," was another with a very influential father. Earl Woods was a teacher, a coach, and a very accomplished golfer in his own right. Earl gave Tiger his first club at seven months, set up his high chair in the garage so that Tiger could watch him hitting balls over and over into a net, and before the age of two, had him at the golf course playing and practicing regularly. Under Earl's tutelage, Tiger maintained a rigorous practice schedule throughout his youth and competed regularly against his peers with good success. In retrospect, however, it took 17 years of intense practice and competition before he finally achieved success at the highest level, when he won the U.S. Amateur at the age of 19. By comparison, U.S. golfing legend Bobby Jones made the quarterfinals in 1916 at the age of 14, three years earlier than Woods even first competed in an event against adults. Now, Tiger obviously went on to set many records in his own right, but very early on his peers on the Tour learned that if they were going to compete with Tiger, they were going to have to practice and prepare their bodies in a way that would compete equally with Tiger's preparation. Prior to his death, whenever Earl Woods was asked the reason for his son's success, he nearly always gave the same answer: it wasn't that Tiger was more talented, it was his hard work.

All of these are examples of individuals who excelled at the highest level in their respective fields, in addition to having an inherent level of talent or God-given gifts that others do not possess. With deeper examination, however, it is obvious that while each obviously possessed the necessary abilities relevant to their chosen profession, it was really their dedication to practicing the things that most effectively increased their performance that set them apart. It was not just practice for the sake of practice, however, that mattered. It was a sort of singular focused practice, designed with the help of coaches to improve the necessary skills that were relevant to success in their fields. So the next time you're headed to the range don't just beat balls with the mindless notion that practice makes perfect. Head out there with a game plan and understanding that you really need to *perfect the art of perfect practice.* You may need to enlist the help of a coach to develop that plan, but either way remember that the perfect practice addresses your deficiencies with the ultimate goal of making them into proficiencies.

OLD HABITS DIE HARD

"A nail is driven out by another nail;
a habit is overcome by habit."
– Desiderius Erasmus

While that saying was uttered over 500 years ago, modern brain science has only recently been able to prove scientifically how insightful the Dutch scholar Erasmus really was. As human beings we are essentially gigantic bundles of habits—habits that are foundational to how we function and get through each and every day. Almost at birth, we begin to develop innumerable habits that help us perform tasks both complicated and mundane, without which we would suffer from having to consciously think about every action we make. Some are habits of action and some of thought, and while some of these habits are good and healthy, others follow the paths of least resistance and subsequently aren't necessarily beneficial.

We develop habits in order to obtain rewards that satisfy cravings that we are often not even consciously aware of. What we generally eat, how much we exercise, how we drive a car, whether or not we are naturally inclined to be positive or negative, are a planner or a procrastinator, and even whether or not we seem to instinctively favor a Republican over a Democrat when election season rolls around is essentially born out of an endless succession of habits that we have been developing since our earliest days.

And many of these habits can have a direct effect on how we play golf. They can determine everything from our level of competitiveness to how nervous we tend to be on the first tee. Even how well or poorly we typically score, in and of itself, can become a habit. The good news is that while these habits can become incredibly embedded over time, if we learn the process of how they work, we can acquire the ability to change and develop new ones regardless of how old we are.

When it comes to changing our golf habits, we need to first discover what they are and how they are affecting our game. This may require a bit of self-analysis, but first it is important to start with an objective perspective. Now, while some people are good at self-diagnosis, it is all too common to be a bit too close to our own problems to have a truly clear picture and understanding of what they are. And while your local PGA professional is a great option when it comes to analyzing your swing habits, there is a group of people a bit closer to home that might be able to give you the keenest insight on what is killing your game: your playing partners.

The people you play with most, if you can get them to be honest, will often have a very clear and unbiased perspective about your game. And while it might at first be humbling, that perspective will likely lead you to very different conclusions than you have drawn yourself. Are you the angry club-thrower, the eternal pessimist, the constantly moaning perfectionist who is never satisfied with even the best of shots, or the overly sensitive type whose rabbit ears seem to pick up potential distractions better than a NASA satellite dish? Get your playing partners to be honest with you, and chances are they even have a nickname for you that they use when you're just out of earshot, which can prove to be very telling about why you struggle at times.

I'm not trying to say that poor swing habits can't at times be the culprit keeping you from improving, but it is our long-standing behavioral habits that we often overlook and can be the hardest to overcome. Be they of the swing type or the behavioral type, though, the common ground between them is that they are truly nothing more than habits—habits that were developed at some point, for some reason, but habits nonetheless. You can replace them with new ones if you have a strong enough desire to do so. And once you have established which habits are affecting your game the most and isolated one that you would like to change, it then becomes important to understand the elements of the habit loop and a typical process for building a new habit to take its place.

In *The Power of Habit*, author Charles Duhigg explains that, for the most part, all habits are comprised of three essential elements: *the cue, the routine,* and *the reward.* To highlight this, let's pick on the last fellow, that overly sensitive guy with the rabbit ears, since you're already somewhat familiar with him from an earlier chapter. Now, we've all played with him (or her) and caught ourselves more than once in anticipation of a rebuke when you accidentally put your club back in the bag, rattling a few of the others, while they were in the midst of a swing. If you were in luck, it was just in the pre-shot and you caught nothing more than a glare as they backed off the ball for the third time on that particular shot. But if you weren't and you caught them mid-swing, the resulting, often profanity-laced undressing you received for being responsible for their fourth water ball of the day was hardly equal to the offense.

So what was the cue? The sound of your club clanking in the bag as you put it away. What was the routine? The obviously overly dramatized acknowledgment of the sound. It needn't be a reaction as over-the-top as I described, but the important part is that ol' rabbit ears let everyone within earshot know that any resulting wayward shot would be directly attributable to the concentration disruption caused by the offending noise. And what was the reward? This is where it can get a little bit tricky. Rewards typically serve to satisfy a craving. In this situation, we'll call the craving a desire for the good opinion of others about his or her golf game and/or a desire to avoid a poor shot that will either embarrass them or at least lower others' opinion of them. This means that the reward for the routine is ultimately the opportunity to abdicate responsibility for a poor golf shot that will cause a blow to his or her ego.

So, assuming they want to, how do our friends with rabbit ears get over their habit of overreacting to every chirping bird, passing car, or rattling club that's within a three-county radius? Scan the multitude of self-help books on the subject and you will find nearly as many suggestions and potential cures out there as there are different types of habits, but modern brain science has now confirmed that his best opportunity for success is to replace that old habit with a new one. Once aware of the cue and having identified the true nature of the reward and the craving it satisfies, they can begin to change the routine. In this case, it is likely he will have to do two things.

The first is to come to terms with the fact that his ability is potentially not at the level he perceives it to be and that, even if it is, no one really earns the good opinion of others by blaming their actions on forces outside of themselves. The second will be to look at each incidence as an opportunity to prove to himself and others that he can accept the responsibility for his actions. And the really funny part is that this replacement habit could potentially bring the actual reward they sought to satisfy their old craving—a newfound respect and admiration from their playing companions, just for a different reason. The cue may still be a sudden, unexpected noise, but in order to achieve the desired reward, he must now adopt a new routine. The new reaction/routine should be planned in advance, require a low amount of activation energy, be very different from the previous routine, and draw little attention to itself. It could be no reaction at all, but *old habits die hard*, and so as long as the resulting action is different, carries little to no emotion, and doesn't require more energy to implement than the previous habit, they will have a far better chance of receiving the desired result. Change doesn't happen overnight, but ultimately the best way to kill an old habit is to start building a new one. And if you're as lucky as ol' rabbit ears, there's a chance that the new one might reward you with what you've been craving all along.

PLAY GOLF, NOT GOLF SWING

"He who aims at perfection in everything
achieves it in nothing."
– Eugene Delacroix

There is a very common problem in the game today,
which seems ever-increasingly fueled by the improvements we
have in technology to teach the game. Access to video and
videotaping swings, as well as software that allows you to
compare your swing to some of the best players in the world has
never been cheaper and more accessible. A big byproduct of this
is an obsession with the idea of perfecting the golf swing. Sure, a
mechanically sound golf swing makes the game easier and more
fun and is a big part of the foundation necessary to take a player
from beginner to average and from good to great, but it is only

one piece of the puzzle. I suppose the fact that swing mechanics have become somewhat of a false idol shouldn't be all that surprising. Blaming our failures on a poor golf swing rather than looking inward at other things (like a lack of confidence, inability to concentrate, or difficulty handling pressure situations) that might be contributing to our inability to get to the next level seems a much easier pill to swallow.

This problem is prevalent with good players—players who seem to have a habitual need to change, refine, and tinker with an already good golf swing in that chase for ever-elusive perfection. And the media's fixation on the mechanics of the golf swing only adds fuel to the fire. You've all seen it. A player hits a wayward shot, particularly down the stretch during a tour event, and the analyst slows down his swing to the millisecond to show us when and where it went wrong and why it caused the shot to take its ill-fated turn. The end result of this type of analysis is that the mass of the golfing public is unintentionally hoodwinked into believing that perfecting their swing is the only path to hitting better shots. They're led to believe that a more mechanically sound swing won't succumb to the pressures of competition and subsequently head to the driving range or their local teaching pro in a quest to get it fixed. If, however, they were really paying attention when watching those golf tournaments, one thing would have become plainly obvious. Even the best golf swings fall prey to nerves and other factors that cause them to fall apart, and there is precious little about the mechanics that will change that fact.

The game of golf is about making shots, not perfect swings, because in truth, as a good teaching professional knows, there is no perfect swing. Each golfer has a swing that they are capable of making based upon their unique physical abilities and limitations, and wrapped inside that is a sense of personal rhythm and tempo, as well as a host of other factors like personality, creativity, self-esteem, and the effects of the culture in which they learned to play the game. All of these factors influence how a golfer swings the club, in a variety of situations, in both subtle and distinctive ways. And a good teacher understands how to interpret these elements and what he or she likely can or can't ask a player to do as a result of them. Becoming wrapped up in a quest for the perfect swing not only has caused many a good player to ultimately lose their game and golf instructors to lose their students, but it is a quest for something that in fact doesn't exist.

The most common and unfortunate byproduct of embarking upon this quest is that players develop the habit of trying to make perfect swings every time instead of hitting golf shots, which shifts their thinking away from the critical right-brain, whose role in creativity is essential in executing specific shots. For example, how often have you hit a drive down the middle of the fairway, only to dump a fairly easy approach into the bunker or somewhere worse? Once the necessity to hit a very specific shot is removed, we often shift from visualizing to trying to just put a good swing on it. That shift results in a switch to the analytical left-brain, whose job it is to judge whether the swing we made meets our definition of perfection and whose very act of analyzing has been proven to disrupt the flow of our well-grooved swings.

Conversely, I am sure you can all remember a time when you hit your tee shot into the woods, leaving you with a very difficult approach that required a ball hit either high or low into a specific spot, with either hook or fade spin on it to get close to or on the green, and you almost amazingly executed it to perfection. In that instance, you had to maintain a precise visualization of the shot you wanted and only then could you free your mind to produce the exact motion needed to make that shot a reality. If the shot is less exacting, like those from the middle of the fairway, your focus can become vague, and the lesser demands free up your mind to wander to the mechanics of your swing, the situation, and the consequences of failing to execute in such a perfect situation. This is why it is important to make it a habit to never stop hitting golf shots, even in practice. It not only prepares you better for playing the game by continually forcing you to execute shots that incorporate more right-brain thinking, but it breaks the cycle of obsessing over the perfect swing. So the next time you play, make a commitment to *play golf, not golf swing*, and you just might be surprised at the shots you hit, especially from the middle of the fairway.

PRACTICE SMARTER, NOT HARDER

*"It's not necessarily the amount of time
you practice that counts, it's what you
put into that practice that counts."*
– Eric Lindros

There are a plethora of books out there these days espousing the merit of the **10,000** hours of practice theory derived from the research of **Dr. Anders Ericsson**. Ericsson's extensive research revealed that, in most every case, elite-level performers, whether they be chess grand masters or athletes, engaged in at least **10,000** hours of practice before they attained success at the highest level in their chosen craft. And while his research was extensive and the results of it have a lot of value to those of us who are occasionally lucky enough to coach an elite-level performer, taking the conclusions of his study at whole cloth can be a bit disheartening for the majority of players who want to improve. The reality is, most of us who play golf (or any other sport, for that matter) do not do so with the expectation of achieving elite-level performance, nor do we have anything near the requisite 10,000 hours to burn. We want to improve so we can enjoy the game even more, but with today's busy lifestyles we want to make sure we get the most out of our practice and the precious time we choose to invest in the process.

In 1906, Italian economist Vilfredo Pareto, after observing that 80 percent of the land in Italy was owned by 20 percent of the population, stumbled upon a nearly universally applicable principle that would come to be named after him some years later. Pareto's Principle, also known as Pareto's Law or the 80-20 rule, would later come to be widely adopted in fields ranging from business to healthcare. It suggests that, in almost any situation, 80 percent of the results are derived from 20 percent of the causes. In business, 80 percent of a company's profits are derived from 20 percent of its customers, 80 percent of the complaints come from 20 percent of the customers, as well, and 80 percent of all sales come from 20 percent of the sales force. In the world of computers, 20 percent of the code written is responsible for 80 percent of the errors and crashes, and 80 percent of Internet traffic occurs during 20 percent of the day. Pareto even observed this ratio in his own garden, at one point finding that 80 percent of the peas came from 20 percent of the pea pods. Again and again, in incredibly disparate situations,

Pareto's Principle has been observed to be uncannily accurate. And when it comes to golf and practice, things are no different.

In the game of golf we are allowed to carry 14 clubs. The array of clubs allowed gives you the ability to hit all sorts of different shots from a myriad of situations and yardages, but the reality of the game is that most golfers hit somewhere between 70 and 80 percent of their shots with about 20 percent (read, *three*) of their clubs. In the majority of cases, those three clubs are the driver, a favorite greenside wedge (typically a sand or lob wedge), and a putter. When you figure most people hit their driver 14 times a round, their favorite wedge 10-15 times a round, and putt about 36 times a round, you end up with about 60-65 actual shots coming from those three clubs. Now throw in the fact that your driver might have caused you a penalty stroke or two or put you in other places a handful of times that you had to hit recovery shots from, and you've got a few more shots. Factor in the likelihood that your favorite wedge left you in the bunker once or twice (or airmailed the green into another bunker) and that your yippy putting stroke makes just two-putting each hole a lofty ambition some days, and you can often find that those three clubs will account for over 70 strokes in a given round. It's no wonder most people play just about as well (and sometimes even better) when courses host a three-club tournament.

Armed with these facts and figures, maybe it's time to take a look at our practice routine. I know, I know, the driving range is so tempting and it's right there (at most clubs, a mere 40 or 50 steps from the clubhouse) and it's so much fun to stand out there for hours upon end beating balls to groove that magical muscle memory, but unless we're doing it with the driver, is that really the best use of our time? And besides, if laziness is part of the excuse, that large expanse of much shorter grass (known as the practice putting green for those of you unfamiliar with it) is generally even closer. And while I know the practice bunker and short game areas are often located way down in the south 40 (often an additional 20 or 30 steps further away), I guarantee that, for a good many of us, the long walk and extra time we invest in taking our favorite wedge for a visit to that area would be an investment that will pay dividends that go way beyond just our waistline.

Now I realize that, for many of you, these comparisons to your own game may not be completely accurate. For some of you, the driver may be the best club in your bag, for others that wedge really is your favorite club, and I'm certain there are at least a few good putters out there. If you do a little 80-20 analysis of your game, however, I can almost guarantee that you will find that about 80 percent of the shots that you throw away during a round come from about three or four clubs in your bag, or at least a handful of specific types of shots. I know this may require a bit of painful introspection to figure out, so the objective eye and analysis of a coach may be necessary, but spend a little time doing it, and I promise you will find out where you should be devoting the most emphasis in your practice routine and how much time you should spend doing it. After all, as precious as all of our time is, the goal should be to *practice smarter, not harder.* And if we can learn to do that, instead of just beating balls until our hands bleed, we might just finally find the path that will lead us to that elusive next level.

EAT, DRINK, AND BE GARY

"The reason fat men are good natured is they
can neither fight nor run."
– Theodore Roosevelt

Not long ago, a member passed on to me an article about Gary Player that profiled his history as a pioneer in golf in the realm of fitness and nutrition. His dedication to making these ideas cornerstones of his life and success earned him the nickname *Mr. Fitness* as far back as the 1950s, and today, at age 77, apparently the nickname still fits. After reading the article, I got to thinking that while I tend to preach proper diet, a healthy lifestyle, and maintaining a modicum of fitness in order to play better and attain your goals, I probably don't really give it its proper due. Now, I realize it is unlikely any of us will start off each day with 1,000 push-ups and sit-ups, as Mr. Player still does, and his largely vegetarian diet will find very few adherents in my neck of the woods, but I do believe the lifestyle Mr. Player ascribes to has some advantages. So let's take a look at a few baby steps we can all take in the way of health and fitness that will help us get an extra edge.

When I was growing up and playing competitively, the idea of working out and leading a healthy lifestyle was nearly on par with blasphemy. "You'll screw up your timing!" "You'll lose flexibility!" "Your distances will be off!" and a slew of other excuses kept us out of the weight room and in the grillroom drinking milkshakes and eating french fries after a round. My how things have changed. Today players on the professional tours have travelling gyms following them from stop to stop, and while Gary Player is widely recognized as the first, Tiger Woods is largely responsible for much of the change in mindset that today's top players (and those aspiring to be one) have in regards to fitness. A slew of golf-related fitness products are now on the market, and a handful of top fitness coaches now work exclusively with golfers, developing routines specific to the needs of athletes playing our sport. If you want an example of the trickle-down effect of this that is closer to home, I can tell you that one of my top students began working with a personal trainer three times a week at the age of thirteen and, as college fast approaches, has upped that number to five.

I understand that the training regimens designed for top athletes aren't a realistic option for most of us, even if we all had the requisite time available to participate in one, but I do believe there are things in the realm of health, fitness, and well-being that we can all adopt into our routines that can ultimately pay dividends on the golf course. So let's take a quick look at the aforementioned subjects and a few areas in which I think you should consider adopting some new related habits, along with some suggestions for doing so.

The first subject is that of diet. If you've got anything close to the french fries and milkshakes habit I had when I was a kid (maybe coffee and doughnuts?), there are likely a few dietary changes that could benefit your game. "You are what you eat," is a statement as venerable as the Old Course at St. Andrews, yet we are only recently beginning to understand just how true that really is. Mr. Player believes nutritionists will be the personal trainers of the future on tour and that diet is about 70 percent of the fitness puzzle.

Our bodies and our dietary needs change as we get older, more often than not requiring us to carry less weight, rather than the few extra pounds many of us annually accumulate around our midsections. If you adopt nothing else from this chapter, reduce or eliminate the amount of sugar, caffeine, and processed foods (most bread, crackers, or anything like them) in your diet, especially just prior to a round. A reduction in caffeine, sugar, and refined processed foods is not only healthy for your body, but it also helps to reduce anxiety and maintain consistent energy levels. In the year 1700, the average American ate five pounds of sugar per year. That number has increased markedly, especially in the past century, to today's frighteningly high number of over 150 pounds per year. From an evolutionary perspective, our bodies haven't had remotely enough time to adjust to that rapid spike. And all those bagels and breads we round out our morning routines with essentially turn into sugar once they hit our bloodstreams, just exacerbating the issue.

As far as drinking goes, sugar isn't the only culprit, and you can likely thank Howard Schultz and the folks at Starbucks for our meteoric rise in daily caffeine intake. Americans now drink more coffee than any other country in the world. And while it certainly doesn't possess as many negative health connotations as sugar, coffee shouldn't exactly be your beverage of choice for a sport in which steady nerves and a relaxed state of mind are beneficial (and most of us drink it with at least a little sugar for good measure). I know, getting rid of your morning cuppa joe might be like swapping your right arm for another left, but if you want a little golf-related story to help support the idea, consider this one. In 1992 Fred Couples won the Masters, capping off the hottest stretch of his career, having won five tournaments plus a couple of silly season events in the previous nine months. To what did he at least partially attribute the streak he went on? Giving up his 12 Cokes per day habit and the resulting sense of calm he felt on the course.

The other problem with drinking, though, is not only what we're drinking, but also what we aren't. Proper hydration is essential for golf and just about everything else in life but is often overlooked, as evidenced by that estimate, mentioned earlier, that

90 percent of Americans are chronically dehydrated. Dehydration obviously can be problematic from a health perspective and is a critically underrated factor in poor sports performance. Why? Well, the brain is 95 percent water, so it is no small wonder that a persistent drought in your cranial region has a negative effect on concentration, focus, anxiety, mood, and our overall sense of well being, even at imperceptibly low levels. So what do most of us do out there to help combat the issue? Have a beer or six or whatever our cocktail of preference may be; this takes an already problematic situation and turns it up to 11 by drinking something else that increases dehydration. If you're shooting for elite-level performance, stick to water as your beverage of choice. Even if you're not and golf is primarily a social outlet for you, mixing in at least a couple of bottled waters during your round, especially on those hot days, can lead to huge rewards.

And finally, we should touch on what is the most stereotypical aspect of being Gary: our level of fitness and what we can do to enable our bodies to perform at a higher level. We all know that we tend to lose strength as we age, especially if we don't do anything to maintain it, but another byproduct of inactivity is a lack of flexibility. That is the No. 1 reason people who come to me can't make the type of golf swing we would like to see. As a result, the primary thing I recommend is a comprehensive stretching routine that you follow at least every other day and prior to rounds of golf. There are numerous products out there like Randy Meyer's Golf Stretching Pole and the slew of products offered by Tour Fitness Coach Joey

DioVisalvi that can help, but stretching can easily be accomplished without the aid of fancy equipment. It's also essential if you want to either continue swinging the same way as you age, or to get back that swing you used to have. Want to build golf-related strength? The Power-Swing Fan is my personal favorite for building your golf-related muscles, but hitting the gym and working with a trainer who at least understands that your strength training must maintain your flexibility is essential. Translation: if weight lifting is your thing, lift less weight and do more reps.

Now being more of a doctor of golf than medicine, I suppose I shouldn't recommend any of this at all without the obligatory, "Consult your physician before embarking on any new fitness and nutrition plan," so consider yourself fairly warned. The reality of the situation, however, is just this. If you haven't yet incorporated fitness and nutrition into your plan to play better golf, then maybe it's time to consider it. We insist on playing the equipment the pros play, the balls they play, and even wearing their brands of clothes in an effort to improve our games, so maybe it's time to start adopting their lifestyles, as well. And in order to do that, we just might need to *eat, drink, and be Gary.* There's a good chance it will improve your game and an even better one it'll improve your health and your life.

PART 5

ON PERSPECTIVE,

JUDGMENT, AND

COMMITMENT

TAKE A LOOK BACK

"Seeking to forget makes exile all the longer; the
secret to redemption lies in remembrance."
– Richard von Weizsäecker

I first learned the game of golf on military and public
courses at an early age. I mostly walked, after nearly putting an
old three-wheeled Harley in the ditch at the McClellan AFB
Course the first time my grandfather, a colonel there, handed me
the tiller. I carried an old canvas bag with one pocket and a
hodge-podge of leather gripped clubs he had cut down for me in
his garage. I played with balls (many with smiles on them) that I
had fished out of the pond on the hole that was adjacent to my
grandfather's backyard or that I had found in the weeds. My
clubs had names like Hagen, Snead, and Littler stamped on
them, and the balls bore names like Club Special, K-28, Dot, and
Kro-Flite when you could read them. I took one group lesson

from a grizzled old pro, which allowed me to get a junior card and play all day (which I did a lot) for $1 at the local three-par. I got invited to play in what would become my first regular foursome when I was about 10 years old by three very patient and good-hearted retired guys who played every day. One of them would give me a dollar for every par I made, and on an average day, I had enough money to buy lunch by the time we finished. He stopped the practice about the time I started making enough pars to buy lunch at the turn. It was a grand game (the best game, I thought), and as it turns out, a pretty good babysitter too, as the most trouble I ever remember getting into was when I accidentally stepped in someone's line prior to learning the proper etiquette. I got my first new set of clubs finally in the seventh grade and I was hooked.

I'm sure that most of you can tell similar stories, and I always love to hear them, but when was the last time you thought about it yourself? There are times we all struggle with our games, and it is at these times that I think it is important to reflect on when and why we started playing golf in the first place and what it was about the game that really grabbed hold of us. I offer proof of this by relating the story of when I first wrote the precursor for this chapter, as it was part of my weekly column. Then, as now, I mentioned the fact that I'd love to hear people's own stories, not expecting how many truly fascinating ones I would receive in return. Here are a few...

There was a woman who, as a teen, carried the clubs of an elderly half-blind neighbor almost weekly for a year, until she was finally frustrated enough just watching other people play that she had to try it herself. There was the attorney who, shortly after passing the bar, got invited by one of his first big potential clients to what he thought was lunch but ended up being a drive to the local country club. Upon their arrival and his question of what in the world they were doing, the client responded with a question of his own.

"You play golf?"

"No," the attorney replied.

"Well, you do now."

Or there was the ex-football star who, after blowing out his knee in college, turned to golf out of boredom during rehab and then, after becoming hopelessly hooked, ended up quitting the team to make golf his career.

I could go on, as the stories I received back were as interesting as they were varied, but the true point of bringing them up is to point out how much people obviously got out of relating them. And while we all started in many different places and for slightly different reasons, most of us started the game with the goal learning to play well enough that we could just have fun ... or at least not embarrass ourselves in the process. Those initial goals were most often aligned with what is referred to as a "mastery approach" as we attempted to become proficient and to learn what it took to play and play well enough to enjoy it. As we improve, however, some of us can lose sight of the ingredients that made us enjoy it so much in the first place—so much that we became addicted. Very often, this coincides with our priorities shifting to playing the game for purposes that are more egocentric. We play for score, for recognition, to enhance those aforementioned business opportunities, to make money, and to look good (or not look bad). Playing from a place that is more egocentric tends to put more pressure on us, as we begin to tie our self-esteem to the score and the results of the game. This can begin to take away from the enjoyment of the game, and the subsequent amount of focus it takes away from learning, improving, and mastering the game in and of itself often leads to our skills taking a step back. It doesn't necessarily have to be this way.

Take a look back to when you started playing golf and on your golfing career as a whole. Was there a time when you were playing better than you are now? Was there a time when you were enjoying it more than you are now? If so, have your priorities, goals, and reasons for playing changed since that time? Is your commitment to improvement in a different place than it used to be? Has the group of players, types of events, or maybe even the situations you play in most often changed? Taking a trip down memory lane has more benefits than just nostalgia. These trips can often reveal clues to why we have ended up where we are, and while we can't exactly turn back the clock, we can learn from our experiences and use this knowledge to begin finding the road back. Golf is a grand game, and like life, it is a journey and even the best players have times when they are frustrated. A little reflection now and then, however, not only is enjoyable, but can go a long way towards making sure that journey leads to getting hooked again! And I truly would love to hear your story: mdowd@oakdalegcc.org.

PUT IT ALL IN PERSPECTIVE

"Everything we hear is an opinion, not a fact.
Everything we see is perspective, not the truth."
– Marcus Aurelius

There are innumerable situations in both golf and life where it can be easy to find ourselves lulled into accepting the narrative of the moment. If we want to grow, however, it is important to develop the habit of taking a step back to question the generally accepted truth. Make it a practice, and you will begin to realize that upon closer inspection those narratives are often nothing more than a collection of similar opinions, not necessarily the truth.

Not long ago I heard a story Hall of Fame pitcher Goose Gossage related to a coach I know who works with Major League

Baseball players on their mental games. And while it's a baseball story, it's a story that I felt couldn't have been more appropriate for athletes in any sport who experience pressure. Like many of us coaches, he was picking Goose's brain for mental game secrets, when Goose told him about the single moment that changed everything in the game for him.

Goose said it happened one day very early in his career. It was the deciding game of a playoff series. It was a "win or go home" situation, and he was nervous and scared. The crowd was going wild, and there were runners on base while his team was clinging to a narrow lead. It was a real defining moment, one that could and likely would define his career for years to come. In the public's eye, he would either be the gutsy young flamethrower with ice water in his veins or a shrinking violet with the inability to rise to the occasion and handle the biggest moments. Well, after throwing an over-amped fastball very high, Goose took a walk around the mound, desperately hoping to find a key to success in the green grass of the infield.

Then for some reason, he asked himself, *What's the worst thing that could happen?*

And he answered his own question: *If we win, we play on. If I blow it and we lose, I'll be fishing tomorrow afternoon. I guess I can handle that.*

And that's when the light bulb went on. *I'll be fine either way*, he thought. With that freedom he stepped back up to the mound and mowed down the rest of the hapless batters he faced that day. He maintained that perspective the rest of his career.

For many of us golfers, we really tend to lose our perspective, and it makes the potential outcome of our shots or scores seem worse than they are. Subsequently, we put much more pressure on ourselves than is appropriate given the situation. We are so concerned with the opinions of others that we tend to forget that they are just opinions, not the real truth about us. Too often, our desire for the good opinion of others and their approval is so pervasive and ever-present that most of us aren't even consciously aware of it. The big problem with this is that it often makes our only real commitment to that of looking good and not embarrassing ourselves. With this type of commitment, it is no small wonder why we feel so much pressure and have so many doubts when we step up to the first tee.

So with all of this in mind, I'd like to suggest that the next time you go out, try and commit to another reason to play. One of the best commitments I know of that will help your game is to play free of doubt or worry. Stop doubting your ability to hit the same shot on the first tee that you just hit 25 times in a row on the driving range. Stop worrying that if you don't, the opinion the hordes of onlookers have of you and your game will be unalterably changed. It isn't easy at first, but if you chose to commit to that instead of trying to look good, it will free you up to make the type of improvement that you might not have thought possible. And to start down this path, the first thing you need to do is *put it all in perspective*. Golf isn't your job, and it doesn't pay your bills (if it does, we might need to introduce you to the handicap chairman). Golf certainly shouldn't be the biggest source of your self-esteem. And do you want a really big shock? No matter how well or poorly you play, no one but yourself will likely care beyond today. And regardless of how big your opinion of the moment is in your own head, what's the worst thing that could ultimately happen? Tomorrow you could be fishing!

COUNTER YOUR CULTURE

"A people without the knowledge of their past, history, origin, and culture are like a tree without roots."
– Marcus Garvey

When you debate the defining factors that explain the dominance of champion golfers and what it takes to make one, there are nearly as many opinions and schools of thought out there as there are swing theories. Whether it be the mechanical prowess of Ben Hogan or Nick Faldo, the mental toughness of Jack Nicklaus or Tiger Woods, the creativity of Seve Ballesteros or Bubba Watson, or the gifted putters like Ben Crenshaw or the early Tom Watson, you find that even the so-called experts have vastly different opinions about what truly separates the men from the boys at the elite level and what element has contributed most to their dominance. Innumerable books have been written about everything from personality types to one's ability to engage the right-brain during performance, yet still the debate rages. A cottage industry has been built around the examination of champion athletes in every sport in an attempt to isolate the reasons for their success, yet curiously, in all of this examination, one incredibly important factor has heretofore been given scant serious consideration up until now—the culture into which they were born, grew up, learned the game, and spent most of their time playing. Examine the following.

I grew up playing and working at a club that had a very distinct culture. It wasn't something that was ever overtly recognized, acknowledged by its members, or decreed in its bylaws, but it was rather, to a certain extent, just a reflection of their collective personalities and values and the way in which the game had been passed on to them. It was a gambler's club, the type of place where nearly everyone had a wager on just about everything, and unlike many clubs, where gambling between staff and club members (or even the younger children of members) was frowned upon, there it was not only accepted, but encouraged. The golf shop opened early each morning to facilitate those who played in the money games, and Fridays and Saturdays were the zenith, with scratch and high-stakes players from nearly every club within a 50-mile radius descending upon the facility to test their mettle against the battle-hardened veterans that called the club home. Morning golf gave way to afternoons and evenings spent on the practice putting green, where money could exchange hands even faster and where the floodlights mounted atop the clubhouse roof allowed games of 5 for $5 and Aces Only to extend into the wee hours of the morning.

The gambling, however, wasn't just confined to the course. Every afternoon the grillroom was crowded, thick with the ever-present haze of smoke from the cigarettes of a generation who had grown up at a time when the hazards of smoking weren't as well understood and the alcohol-induced din of half a hundred voices. The ladies played Gin (and drank it too), the guys Cribbage, Guts, or Liar's Dice, all while the more serious gamblers filled the poker tables in the men's locker room, playing until the smoke cleared and everything paused around 5:00 or 6:00 P.M., just long enough for everyone to go home, get a bite of dinner, and sleep a bit before it began anew the very next day. There was a fantasy football league, football pools every Sunday during the season, giant Super Bowl pools, March Madness pools, Masters pools, and so on. There were twice-weekly $5 pools for the winning numbers in the lottery, and pari-mutuel wagering was a part of nearly every event, with the professional staff being consulted in much the same way handicappers are at the track before each and every horserace. Gambling was not only ever-present and pervasive, it was the culture, so it was not surprising when, upon finding his cart staff killing time in the bag room one afternoon, wagering $1 for each ball successfully lobbed over a water pipe and into an awaiting bucket of water in one bounce, the head professional didn't get angry—he joined in the game.

It was a culture in which the art of the hustle was glorified and terms like *negotiations, propositions,* and *parking lot split* dominated the lexicon. At one point I even ran an annual tournament called "The Big Hustle," my co-chair being a guy who had paid cash for his first car at the age of 16 with money he had been hustling off the members since the age of nine. Taking all this into consideration, it wasn't the least bit surprising when one day I overheard two of the club's more notorious members in a discussion where one said, "You know we're gonna have to let Joe win today, don't you? He's a pigeon for sure, but if we don't throw him a little bread today, that pigeon's gonna fly away!" In retrospect, it was country club golf's version of the Wild West, a near lawless and often morally bankrupt environment of swindlers, hustlers, gamblers, and thieves. And it was where I learned to play.

In a culture like that one, a culture that values the wager more than what you are wagering on, the game becomes secondary, and it is no small wonder that a certain type of golfer emerges from that environment. Not surprisingly, the nearly universally preferred game was a scramble. The golf calendar revolved around three events: the Oldsmobile Scramble, a Scratch Two-Man Scramble, and the Men's Invitational (one round of which was a scramble), and every Tuesday night during daylight saving time, there was a Nine-Hole ABCD Scramble where each player put $25 in the pot and the winners took all. In some circles, scrambles are considered a near sacrilege to the game, the domain of beer-guzzling hackers in flip-flops and tank tops or the preferred format of charity golf events designed to compensate for the propensity those events have for attracting once-a-year players who need all the help they can get just to get around in less than six hours. It's a bastardization of the game that no more resembles real golf than the type played with windmills and clown's mouths. At this club, however, scrambles allowed for and essentially encouraged a style of play that was high-risk and high-reward. Poor shots went largely un-penalized, encouraging a go-for-broke mentality that doesn't translate well when it comes to the real golfing world of stroke play. Add in the additional payoff for Bullets (an extra $1 for any putt made outside the length of the flag), and you have the recipe for a specific type of player. One who could hit it off the planet long and putt the eyes out of the ball but who engaged in a very risky style of play. I grew up playing with a lot of guys like this. They weren't the steady players who lull you to sleep with a ho-hum even par round, because pars didn't pay. They were more likely to shoot 77 or 80, but they did it in swashbuckling fashion, with five bullet birdies and an eagle, but plenty of bogeys and doubles sprinkled in for good measure, because that is what brought home the bread. In retrospect, all these cultural factors form a legacy that shaped how I learned to play the game, one I haven't ever really shed, and it is unfortunately still very much how I find myself instinctively playing today.

This brings me back to the discussion of culture and how it shapes players into champion golfers. The age-old argument of nature vs. nurture has ever been debated when champion golfers are examined, with the nature argument typically winning out. Sure, it is generally conceded that the better golfers in the world have had great instruction, as many of their instructors have gone on to become nearly as famous as they are, but the prevailing notion has ever been that champion golfers are more born than they are made; it is just their nature. It is something about their internal wiring that just makes them different, and someone like Tiger Woods has only led to the advancement of this thought process. Having won golf tournaments with four different swings and major tournaments with three, many even high up in the profession steadfastly hold to the belief that Tiger would have won regardless of what swing he had used and who was teaching it to him. He's just different.

But if that is true, what made him so different? To the greatest degree, I believe it was his culture. And while I've already discussed some elements of Tiger's upbringing, let's take a look at it through a slightly different lens. I think you will see how a unique blend of cultural factors formed deep roots in Tiger prior to when he first burst on the national scene in the late 1990s. Consider collectively the parents he was born to, how they raised him, his early teachers (Rudy Duran and Butch Harmon), his very early exposure to the media (on national television at age three), the clubs like Torrey Pines that he played regularly and had access to, the myriad of events he consistently played in to test his mettle against his peers, as well as the amount of time he was afforded to put in the thousands of hours of practice necessary to achieve the level of mastery at his craft it would take to excel.

Tiger was born as the only child of mature parents with the time, flexibility, and desire to make him their sole priority, and he started playing the game before he was two and was being coached professionally by the age of four. Tiger's mother was Asian and instilled in him the lessons and disciplines of Buddhism at a time long before its tenets were widely taught by the best mental game coaches to aspiring champion golfers. Factor in his ethnicity, the mental toughness that came from being somewhat of an outsider in the world of golf, as well the toughness passed onto him from a father who was a devoted athlete in his own right, an accomplished coach of young men, and a military man who embedded in Tiger the values of discipline and unending hard work to achieve success, and you start to paint a picture. All things considered, it would have been, to a certain degree, more remarkable if Tiger *hadn't* achieved a high level of success in the game. Sure, Tiger was skilled, but he was extremely fortunate, as well. Remove any one of the significant cultural factors Tiger was born into (his mother, father, ethnicity, his early media exposure, or his access to some of the best facilities and teaching in the game), and it is likely he wouldn't have had near the level of success that he has. Provide any one of the thousands of promising young golfers out there exposure to a similar cultural environment, and they would very likely experience a higher degree of success, as well.

So when it comes to understanding your game and why you have particular strengths and weaknesses, try taking a look at the culture in which you were introduced to the game, where you learned to play, and from whom. Think back to the types of games you typically played in, what was most valued, and who and what you played for. Then look at the culture and environment you play the game in now and the types of games you find yourself most often playing in. I'm not suggesting you need to take a Freudian trip to your unconscious mind and uncover every missed two-foot putt buried deep within your psyche, but rather a look at the overall conditions that are responsible for the type of golfer you are today. Taken together, all these things just might reveal a few clues to why you've struggled in the past and/or your natural playing tendencies and why you might have developed them. Then all you need to do is learn to *counter your culture*. It may be difficult at first, as the conditions and tendencies developed by our culture can at times seem to have us forever anchored like the deep roots of a mighty tree, but we can change, and a newfound self awareness might be what you need to take those first steps. And if you do so, you just might find they are the steps up to the next rung on the ladder of your future success.

SHOOT FOR YOUR PERSONAL PAR

"A man's got to know his limitations."
– Clint Eastwood as Harry Callahan

Did you know that less than 1 percent of all golfers have ever finished an 18-hole round at a regulation golf course in par or better? In light of this, the concept of par might be one of the most diabolically conceived aspects of the game of golf and could arguably be called its biggest single source of frustration (outside of slow play). There is very little about the relative difficulty of each course that we play that is taken into account when computing the par. Additionally (and more importantly), the differing abilities of each player and how far they hit the ball aren't a consideration, either. Scottish golf history tells us the term par dates from late 19th-century England. It gained popularity in the U.S. in the early 1900s and was adopted by the

USGA in 1911, along with a relatively sadistic system for computing par based upon hole yardages. Under this system, par is determined by assigning uniform playing lengths for holes for *scratch golfers* of each gender. This is represented in the table below.

Par	Men (Yards)	Women (Yards)
3	Up to 250	Up to 210
4	251 to 470	211 to 400
5	471 to 690	401 to 590
6	691+	591+

This system then assumes these same scratch golfers will take two putts on each hole, and added to that will be the number of shots it should take him or her to reach the green. Now, I'm all for high standards, but looking at this I think you can see the folly in most of us consistently measuring our games against a standard that is all but unattainable. Golf is a difficult game. Maybe the most difficult, and by painting everyone with such a broad brush when it comes to par, you are essentially measuring 99 percent of the players against the best 1 percent that has ever played. Not only that—golf is known as the game of a lifetime, with regular players of both genders playing from almost the time they can stand up until sometimes into their 90s, and to assume that, whether you're 9, 29, or 90, you have the ability to hit the ball as far as a scratch golfer is downright ludicrous. It might not have been conceived this way intentionally, but under the current system of computing par, haven't we essentially set most everyone up for failure?

The game of golf has been scrambling around the past half-dozen years or so to try and figure out why it has been losing players. The amount of time it takes to play, an unfriendly environment towards women and children, too restrictive dress codes, too expensive equipment, too many rules, the recession, and other reasons have all been targeted as contributory factors in the slight decline in participation. At the same time, many in the game's leadership have been lamenting the fact that more of today's youth aren't even picking it up in the first place. The shorter time commitment, faster pace, and lower initial investment to participate in sports like soccer, basketball, and tennis are constantly cited as reasons our nation's youth are opting for those other sports, while the allure of ever increasingly realistic video games is bemoaned as the single biggest factor keeping kids from even participating in sports period. Certainly there can be cogent arguments made for all of these issues as potential barriers to increasing participation in the game, but could a big part of the problem be hidden in plain sight?

The fact is, most people of any generation aren't generally inclined to stick with something very long if they aren't very good at it or don't at least see some improvement in their ability. So when it comes to the game of golf, our forefathers may have inadvertently set the bar so high that, for the majority, significant improvement will never be possible. And while even though misery apparently loves company (and we've got a lot of company here), most people aren't likely to keep doing something if they are (by the industry standard, at least) miserable at it! If you want new people to become attracted to the game in the first place, an ever-present air of impossibility isn't necessarily the best impression to give off.

So here is what I am suggesting. First of all, don't get me wrong—the concept of par is a good one, and it has served us fairly well for a long time. It just needs a little tweaking. Secondly, I am always one for preserving the game's traditions, it's just that in the quest to attract more players, keep more players engaged, and allow the majority of us the opportunity to enjoy the game more and stay motivated on our quests to improve, I think we are long past the time when we should have updated it a bit so that everyone who plays has a better measuring stick to gauge their games. To accomplish this, we need to bring par up to the 21st century, so I've developed a new chart upon which each player has the ability to find their *personal par*; instead of being gender-based, it will be based upon how far each player is able to carry their average drive in the air.

Tier	Drive Carry (Yards)	Par 3 (Yards)	Par 4 (Yards)	Par 5 (Yards)	Par 6 (Yards)	Par 7 (Yards)
5	Up to 100	0 to 100	101 to 200	201 to 300	301 to 400	401+
4	100 to 150	0 to 125	126 to 250	251 to 375	376 to 500	501+
3	150 to 200	0 to 175	176 to 350	351 to 475	476 to 600	601+
2	200 to 250	0 to 225	226 to 450	451 to 575	576+	N/A
1	250+	0 to 275	276 to 550	551+	N/A	N/A

Now, please believe me—I totally get that for many purists the idea of par-sixes is near blasphemous, let alone par-sevens, but if you carry this logic forward a bit, I think you can see the method to my madness. Aside from male professionals and the best men amateur players out there today, virtually no one hits the ball 250+ yards in the air off the tee, so almost no one should be playing under the current par structure. The average man carries his tee shot a little over 175 yards in the air, and the average woman less than 150. This would mean the average regulation course would likely end up playing to a regulation par of somewhere in the high 80s for the average man and of a little over 100 for the average woman. Is it now any small wonder why the average men's and ladies' handicaps have hovered around 18 and 32 respectively for decades?

Measuring par on my chart has a host of other potential benefits, as well. Remember the slow play issue? One of the biggest contributors to that problem has long been players who are playing from the wrong set of tees for their given ability. Extra strokes equals extra time and less fun, so instead of assigning players to tees by handicap or gender, you could assign them by which Tier Tee is most appropriate for how far they hit the ball. Ideally more and more clubs would eventually have up to five different sets of tees, but with everyone playing at least from the set that allows them the best opportunity to shoot their *personal par*, you will cut strokes and time off everyone's round. This could allow for players of differing ages and genders to compete on a more level playing field, opening up the door for new and different types of events.

Now, I can already hear your gears turning, so trust me, I get the fact that this would open up a whole can of worms when it comes to handicapping, and I can already hear the cries of "Sandbagger!" when you get paired with another Tier 3 guy in the Men's Invite and he hits three or four drives over 200 yards, all the while crying, "I don't know what's got into me today, I've never hit it this good." The real point is this: the majority of golfers aren't scratch players, so the game and the majority of its players need a more accurate litmus test to measure their ability. Can't we all agree it would be more fun to have a standard to shoot for that is potentially attainable? I'll leave the handicapping aspect to the rocket scientists (I know one actually and might just put it to him), but if you at least use the chart I created to establish what *your* par should be on the course you play and from the set of tees you play most often, you can finally get a realistic number to shoot for, and it will be a much better measuring stick by which to gauge your day-to-day rounds. So *shoot for your personal par* and in a sense you will be playing the course (in relation to par, at least) much the same way that the pro or scratch player does every day. And because of that I think you'll find that how you feel about each and every round is a lot more positive—in the end, doesn't that sound like a whole lot more fun?

MAKE CONCENTRATION A FASCINATION

"The secret of concentration is the
secret of self-discovery."
– Arnold Palmer

Not long ago, I was at a teaching symposium where renowned instructor Fred Shoemaker related a story to the group. A few years ago, when he was speaking to a large gathering of golf professionals (both teaching and playing), he asked them to share what they believed to be the most important factor in playing great golf. Predictably, there was initially a long list of ideas, so they were asked to narrow it down. Now, I feel obligated to tell you that golf professionals can debate whether or not the sun is up, but after much discussion, this group was able to whittle down the list until at last they arrived at a single critical factor: concentration.

In the next breath, he asked how many of them gave lessons in concentration. No hands went up. He then asked how many of them had ever taken a lesson in concentration. Again no hands went up... So apparently we have in the game a great conundrum. Our best and brightest agree that the single most important factor in playing great golf is not only something that they aren't even teaching, but something they have never even taken a lesson in themselves. When you consider this, I guess it's not that surprising that the average handicap hasn't gone down in over 30 years.

So if concentration is so important, then the obvious next question is, *What can we do to start improving our powers of concentration?* One of the most effective ways I've found is a practice that has been taught by Gurus the world over for centuries, and it combines an intention to change along with awareness. Most of us over the age of 40 love to gripe about the short attention span of today's youth, but I can attest to the fact that the average golfer's ability or inability to focus rivals anything we see from young people. The golf swing only lasts about two seconds on the average, a mere blip in the scope of time but an excruciatingly long time to keep one's attention on any one thing when you really want to. *Don't pull it! Stay relaxed! Don't embarrass yourself! What's for dinner? Keep your head down! Will you ever shut up?* This is just a small sampling of what that little voice in our head is telling us in the small space of time between drawing the club back and impact, and the first step towards change is just to pay attention to what actually is being said in that little internal conversation. Doing this will highlight whether it is mostly positive or negative, and if it's the latter, make it your first intention to change the tone.

If multiple instructions are going on, as they likely are, or they are mostly negative (or attempts to *not* do something), you begin to reduce them one at a time by just noticing when they are there and making a note of it. Examples of negative instructions are, "Stay away from that O.B. on the left!" "Try not to screw up!" or "Don't dump it in the bunker again!" If at any point you notice these little monsters starting to creep in, you can begin to chase them away by giving them more attention or, better yet, by replacing them with those that are a conscious attempt to actually *do* something. "Swing smooth!" "Slow down!" or even "Grip it and rip it!" are, while maybe not the most ideal swing thoughts, at least a positive attempt to actually do something (rather than *not* do something) and should at least be given more space than any of the aforementioned negative ones.

The next thing to try is to make it your conscious intent to pay attention to the target and whether or not you can keep the image of it in your mind once you look back at the ball to begin your swing. If, like a lot of us, the ball creates interference that causes you to lose your connection to the target, tighten up, give yourself instructions, or begin that little conversation in your head again, then start the process over. Stick with the process for long enough (at least a dozen times or so) to see if you can gradually improve your ability to keep the image of the target in your mind while looking at the ball. If the ball is still too powerful, though, try hitting some chips or putts just looking at the target rather than the ball for a while and notice the differences. The point is *to make concentration (or your lack thereof) a fascination.* Be curious, play around a bit, and pay attention to when you lose it, when you get it back, and what causes you to do so. As Arnie said, the secret to concentration is self-discovery, and this fascination with and heightened awareness of what's really going on during those brief moments just prior to and during your swing will begin changing things without you even realizing it. It's only a starting point, but think of it this way—you've now had more lessons in concentration than 99 percent of the golf pros out there.

SWING ONE WAY, JUST ONE DAY

"Until one is committed, there is hesitancy, the chance to draw back, always ineffectiveness."
– William Hutchison Murray

One of the toughest virtues in life to adhere to is commitment. I have heard commitment defined as making a goal and sticking to it with dedication, determination, and optimism regardless of the obstacles. Obviously desire is a key factor in motivation and accomplishing any goal, but it is that unrelenting dedication to staying with a course of action despite the ups and downs that generally determines success or failure. Learning this and believing the wisdom in it can be important to success in many areas of life, but in golf commitment is particularly important when it comes to trusting your swing—

something most of us golfers are unfortunately often guilty of not doing. Failure to trust your swing is likely one of the single biggest factors in why some shots go awry and others don't. A lack of commitment creates hesitancy when standing over the ball, saps your confidence, and leaves you in a situation where even though you may physically go through with it, you often aren't 100 percent mentally committed to the swing you are making.

On the course, a lack of commitment results in us changing our swings, our routines, our swing thoughts, or even our whole approach after every poor shot. I'm not suggesting that if you've shanked the last seven balls or topped five tees shots in a row that a visit to your local PGA professional isn't in order; I'm talking about the habitual tinkering a great many of us engage in after something goes even slightly awry. Some of this can be attributable to the culture of swing mechanics the media has cultivated, which I've already mentioned. When we are bombarded by television and print media that lead us to believe that nearly every poor shot is a result of some flaw in a player's swing, it's no small wonder that we would want to change something, anything. If the TV analysts with their ultra slow-motion replay and the top-100 instructor writing his latest piece in *Golf Digest* both keep telling us that it's some deep-seated mechanical flaw or a less than perfect swing that resulted in our ball going into the woods, then it's unsurprising that every time we hit one of those shots, we are looking around desperately for the culprit. The unfortunate side effect of this is that it causes many of us to fall into the trap of habitually changing our swing or our approach during a round.

The other likely reason for this knee-jerk reaction is just the culture of human nature and maybe Einstein's age-old definition of insanity. You remember it: "Doing the same thing over and over again and expecting a different result." We are hard-wired to want to solve problems, and staying the course in any situation when something isn't working seems less than proactive. If our car isn't running right, we fix it or have it fixed. If our lawn goes brown in one area each summer, we adjust the sprinklers or aerate. If our marriage is on the rocks, we go to counseling. The list is endless, but the fact is, when something isn't working, we instinctively want to make a change and do something to fix it. The idea to just keep on keeping on rarely *feels* like the path to *any* solution.

The problem with this, however, is that constantly shifting your approach breeds a lack of trust in all previously made decisions. If you have come to be so convinced that, every time something goes awry, there is an inherent flaw in your approach, you will find it nearly impossible to play with much confidence. For even the best players, things go wrong in golf more than they go right. Golf is a fickle game, with a club approaching the ball at speeds close to and sometimes over 100 miles per hour, where even a 2 percent deviation in face angle at impact can result in a ball travelling 50 to 60 yards offline. With that in mind, it's easy to understand why our poorest swings are very often a result of pressure and a mental breakdown rather than inherent flaws in the mechanics. Not swinging freely, getting quick, holding on too long, and not allowing the club to release are excuses you hear that apply to players of every level and are almost always a result of a player that is hesitant, fighting doubts about their approach, or not trusting their swing.

This is when having a strong sense of commitment can really help. Doing the same thing over and over again, despite what happens, can actually inspire a sense of confidence and calm the mind. *Swing one way, just one day* is something I love to preach to my most competitive students. This means commit to your routine and to your swing for an entire round regardless of results. Everyone hits shots (a lot of shots), even tour players, that come off less than how we intended, but that doesn't mean we should throw the baby out with the bathwater by trying to change something every time we hit one a little wayward. Accept a poor shot for what it is—just a poor shot. That same swing has likely produced many successful shots, as well, so keep it in perspective and accept that it's just part of the cycle. Recommit to your routine and trust your swing, and it will likely repay you with a shorter amount of time before the next good shot. It will be hard at first. You might not be able to make it even nine holes. Stick with it anyway. Because if you can learn to *swing one way, just one day*, one day you just might find out how truly effective the swing you have really is.

PART 6

ON PATIENCE,

PERSEVERENCE, AND

COMPOSURE

SLOW DOWN

"Patience is not simply the ability to wait, but how we behave while we're waiting."
– Joyce Meyer

If you've been paying attention at all, you've likely noticed how in vogue it is these days to rant about the ills of slow play and how much it is hurting our industry. I think they've missed the point. Golf has always been a slow game, appropriately slow. So while the rest of golf's leadership is spending a great deal of time and resources combating slow play's causes and suggesting potential cures, I'm sure many of you might instinctively think that I've gone over to the dark side for even mentioning anything to the contrary. Hear me out for just a moment, though, and promise to keep an open mind. In the end I believe there's at least a small chance you'll agree with what I have to say or, at the very least, gain a slightly different perspective on the whole pace-of-play issue in golf today.

With campaigns like the USGA's "While We're Young" and the PGA's "Golf 2.0" putting the pace of play in today's game front and center, one could easily get the impression that modern golf has evolved into a proverbial death march. But could it actually be that the pace of our golf is perfectly appropriate? Could there be even a small chance that we might need to learn to make the pace of our busy lives adapt to the pace of the game, rather than trying to make the pace of the game adapt to us? Are we beating our heads against the wall by insisting that we need to improve the pace of play so that more people can squeeze a round of golf into their hectic schedules? Maybe each of us should be taking a hard look at why we find it difficult to set aside the appropriate amount of time to relax and enjoy a round of golf. I won't pretend to suggest that I have the answer to all these questions, but if you at least consider some of the following, you just might think about things a little differently the next time you're stuck behind a group that you'd swear teed off somewhere prior to the Nixon Administration.

Golf is an inherently slow game. Despite golf carts, GPS devices, and all our best efforts, the fact remains that the average 18-hole round at the average par-72 course still clocks in at just over four hours. And while we actually only engage in the playing part of the game for 15 to 20 minutes during those hours, we still have all that in-between time getting from point A to point B over a near-five-mile landscape. And we do that all while looking for lots of errant golf shots, deliberating over the merits of a 7-iron versus an 8-iron (when we really need a 5 into that two club wind), discussing the merits of Callaway versus TaylorMade, arguing about whether the Democrats or the Republicans are to blame for the mess in Washington, and even occasionally admiring the often awe-inspiring beauty of the idyllic settings we find ourselves in. This doesn't even take into account the potential business deals we might be striking, the dormant friendships we are often rekindling, the life lessons to our children we are hopefully teaching, and the all-important quality time with our spouses and significant others we are spending, discussing everything from the grocery lists to the mortgage to the health of aging parents whose future we must now decide upon in one of life's most ironic role reversals. All of these things are important things. Time well spent and invested. And in today's busy life, a round of golf is often one of the few times and places we slow down long enough to have these conversations.

And the advent of those modern golf carts and GPS devices hasn't helped the matter as much as we'd like to believe. Golf used to be played primarily by men and women who traversed those miles on foot. And for those of us who had trouble lugging a 20-pound bag of sticks over that landscape or figuring out the distance from point A to point B, there were caddies. While it definitely took longer to get from shot to shot when we walked, amazingly, the group in front of us was very often gone by the time we got there. Don't get me wrong—golf carts are here to stay, and they can allow many golfers to extend their playing careers years beyond when they would be forced to hang up the spikes if required to walk, but they also have created a big part of the perception problem when it comes to pace of play. The *hurry up and wait* phenomenon.

Yes, golf carts allow us to get to the ball much more quickly, but the game is not yet a polo match. Last time I checked, you actually had to stop and get out of that golf cart to strike the ball, not to mention wait for the group in front of you to do the same. Some of the street-legal carts I see driving around go more than 30 miles per hour, but the problem with that, psychologically, is much the same as what people experience in stop-and-go traffic. We hate waiting, and many of us, when faced with a similar situation in our cars, will actually take a longer route to get somewhere if we know it affords us the opportunity to drive straight through without stopping. It's a peculiar quirk of human psychology and a likely byproduct of our fast-paced lifestyle. It's one of the largest factors in road rage, so it's no small wonder that similar little episodes on the golf course often end with someone hitting into the group in front of them to quote "send a message." I know we aren't likely turning back the clock to a time when people walked the world's courses more than they rode, but it is more than a little curious that pace of play isn't nearly as big of an issue at many clubs in the U.K., where the majority of players still walk.

And how much have those other modern technologies we have at our disposal really helped? The smartphones and GPS devices that have made all of our lives so much easier in so many ways have also done their fair share to contribute to our issues. Sure, we can get a much more exact yardage to the flag these days, without walking it off from the nearest marker, but we can also track the distance from shot A to shot B, track how far each club goes, how far it is from every conceivable hazard on the course, and even check the slope and wind direction if we really want (throwing up a few blades of grass was just too hard). All this on a little handheld device that sometimes feels like it takes an advanced degree from MIT to operate. And with our smartphones, we are now connected to the pro shop, the beverage cart girl, the snack bar, and the rest of the world unlike anytime before. Once upon a time, I can remember playing a spirited game of knobs (or blocks) when we found ourselves waiting on the tee, but now we are more likely calling the pro shop to complain, conducting a little business, checking the scores of the game, posting to Facebook, or any myriad of other things when we're waiting on a slower group, none of which really involves actually engaging with our playing partners.

Now with all this in mind, I think we need to really take a hard look at why we are playing in the first place and figure out why we are in such a hurry. Isn't being on the golf course, after all, one of those well earned rewards that we've all worked so hard for? Has the stress, fast pace, and perceived time famine of the modern lifestyle become so great that we can't at least mentally step off the merry-go-round during those times we've set aside to do just that? Has the thought of actually stopping to smell the roses (or fresh-cut grass in our case) become so cliché that we merely nod and pay homage to it as the quaint notions of a time long past? I hope not, for if we cannot slow down long enough to enjoy and engage in the most important reasons we are out there in the first place, then our game might actually be in trouble.

Studies done by the **PGA** of America have determined that the vast majority of players play the game for reasons mostly aligned with its social aspects rather than anything related to competition. So if we are trying to eliminate or at least mitigate those elements of our game in the hopes of reducing the amount of time we are out there, are we not potentially alienating the largest part of the game's participants by eliminating the reasons they play in the first place? I know there are other factors that contribute to these issues, but the next time things *slow down* out there, I hope you will stop at least momentarily and consider what about this game is most important to you and where you're really in such a hurry to get to. And in the spirit of that, the following is my adaptation of a little poem titled "Slow Dance," by psychologist David L. Weatherford. I call it "Slow Down." And for your sake I hope it doesn't resonate too loudly.

Have you ever taken out a kid for their first round,
or played through the rain, slapping on the ground?
Ever followed your ball's erratic flight?

Or do you just look away, disgusted at the sight?

You better slow down, don't play so fast.

Time is short, this round won't last.

Do you race through each round on the fly?

Ask a partner how are you, but not hear their reply?

When the round is done do you lie in your bed,

with only bad shots running through your head?

You'd better slow down, don't play so fast.

Time is short, this round won't last.

Ever told your child, I'm late for my game, we'll play tomorrow?

And in your haste, not see his sorrow?

Ever lost touch, let your old foursome die?

Cause you couldn't find time to play or at least call and say hi?

You'd better slow down, don't play so fast.

Time is short, this round won't last.

When you try to play so fast just to get somewhere,

you'll miss most of the fun of getting there.

When you worry and hurry through your round each day,

it's like an un-opened gift thrown away.

This game is not a race, do take it slower,

and figure out why you're really out there before the round is over.

Slow down.

BE PATIENT TO A POINT

"Patience and perseverance have a magical effect before which difficulties disappear and obstacles vanish."
– John Quincy Adams

I was on the driving range one day when someone asked me how long I thought that a student should work with an instructor before they really saw results. This is a great question and one that has a lot of implications, but upon reflection, I think my instinctive first answer was a little misleading. I am always hesitant to say anything critical of another instructor and his or her lack of progress with a student, because I understand how rare and difficult successful changes really are and how unrealistic most students' expectations are. Real changes in the golf swing require both patience and perseverance, something typically in short supply among both students and instructors, particularly in this day and age of instant gratification and our *What have you done for me lately?* culture.

"Oh, about 18 months," I said with only a hint of a smile.

"That long?" he asked, with a note of desperation in his voice.

"Well, when you look at all the best players in the world that have undergone major swing changes—Nick Faldo, Greg Norman, and Tiger Woods, to name a few—that is about the average amount of time before they could play to the level they were at before they decided to make swing changes." I continued, "And those guys worked diligently and tirelessly at implementing those changes." Now while I was talking to a very good player, I wasn't talking to a tour player. I realize in retrospect that the impression that I left was inadvertently inaccurate and that my answer was incomplete and inadequately addressed his concerns, but it has caused me since to really think about the nature of students' expectations and what they have a right to realistically expect when they embark upon taking lessons with an instructor.

Affecting change in the golf swing, in truth, requires a handful of elements to be successful. The first are the student's responsibility, and these are the desire to improve, a willingness to make the necessary prescribed changes, realistic expectations about the pace of improvement, and the dedication to work long enough and diligently enough that the changes become embedded to the point of being second nature. The second group of factors are in the instructor's control, and these are an in-depth knowledge of the golf swing, an ability to analyze a player's swing and recognize the elements of it that are most in need of change, an ability to communicate those changes in a variety of ways to players of every level with a variety of learning styles, and finally a level of enthusiasm, confidence in their ability, and engagement in a player's success that will keep a player motivated even when progress is slow. It is no small feat, and it is amazing how infrequently these elements all align, yet if any of them is absent, real change is unlikely, and the result is typically frustration for both student and teacher.

Earlier in my career, I was fortunate enough to have one student who met all the required elements that we instructors hope for. She came to me as a beginner with a 50 handicap, knowing little about the game, but with the desire to improve, the willingness to learn and change, and the time and inclination to work diligently on everything I asked her to. She even had a fair amount of hand-eye coordination and so was, in many ways, a dream student. In about 18 months, she went from that 50 handicap to playing in the mid-teens (which is pretty good on a long golf course where the ladies' tees were pretty much an afterthought) and ultimately challenged for the ladies' club championship. Along the way she listened intently to everything I said and worked patiently to implement it, but mostly she worked hard, often practicing and playing five to six days a week for as much as six to eight hours a day. Ultimately, while I like to believe my guidance was important, she got out of it what she put into it, and given her commitment, I am not hesitant to say that she would have likely achieved as much with any number of instructors guiding her. Seeing her vast improvement, however, many a student came to me in the years immediately following, hoping I could do the same for them. And when they asked me to, I always responded in the same way: "Are you really willing to change and committed to working as hard as she did?"

This brings me back to my initial response to that good player out here at my club not long ago. *How long should you work with someone before you should expect to see results?* Well, now I think I should have followed that question with a question. "How long have you been working with your instructor, and how hard have you been working?" would have been a better answer. In truth, 18 months is a long time, and while I was answering a very good player who had the desire to become great, the level of the player and the goal is relative. Any student of any level should go into working with an instructor with a level of expectation that is in line with their level of commitment.

Real change often, unfortunately, results in a player going a little backwards before they start to move forward, but if a student is making an honest effort at implementing the prescribed changes, they should at least begin to see glimpses of what those changes can do for them after a handful of sessions. These glimpses will typically show up on the driving range first. And then, if the student is patient, slowly but measurably the trust in those changes will begin to take hold, and results will show up on the golf course. But a student should only be patient to a point. If the commitment is there and numerous sessions or months have gone by without any real glimpses of that light at the end of the tunnel, then maybe it's time for a change. Patience is important, but life is short, and if you've persevered, at least to a point, it might not necessarily be a bad message, but that you just need a new messenger. And a true instructor should be as committed to your improvement as you are and should enthusiastically support you in your quest to improve.

P.S. I originally wrote this as part of my column a little over two years prior to this printing. That good player I mentioned left his previous instructor shortly after our conversation, and we started working together in an effort to help him reach his goals. I am happy to report that his hard work, patience, and perseverance ultimately resulted in him winning our Men's Club Championship last summer.

PLAN TO PERSEVERE

"Many of life's failures are those who didn't realize how close they were to success when they gave up."
— Thomas Edison

I was reminded of this quote not long ago upon reading the book *The Grand Slam, Bobby Jones, America, and the Story of Golf.* It is a voluminous tome that is nearly 20 hours long (in the audio book format that is my preferred way of reading these days), which chronicles not only the life of Jones, but also the history of how the game evolved in this country in the earliest days of the 20th century. Being a history buff, I found it an absolutely fascinating read and one that I highly recommend. The research that author Mark Frost undertook to be able to describe matches that took place nearly 100 years ago in the blow-by-blow fashion that he does and the very personal moments that inhabit the space surrounding them was expansive and really makes you feel as if you were actually there. His writing is remarkably reminiscent of the legendary sports writers of that era, like O.B. Keeler, Grantland Rice, and Herbert Warren Wind. Frost also masterfully depicts that while the clothes and the equipment might have been a bit different at the time, the essence of the game and the challenges it presents us all remain unchanged.

Edison's quote came to mind upon reading it because of how incredibly close Bobby Jones came to quitting competitive golf nearly a decade before achieving the now-legendary and unparalleled Grand Slam. Jones was a prodigal junior player who broke 80 before the age of 10 and who finished runner-up in his first national championship, the U.S. Amateur, at the age of 14. His mixture of power and finesse had earned him a reputation that preceded him, but his nearly uncontrollable temper did, as well, and almost derailed his career before it started. The stress of competition, a reprimand by the USGA after a thrown club hit a woman spectator, and the disappointment of failing to live up to the promise of his early potential had begun to take a toll on him by his early twenties and had aged him beyond his years. He began contemplating whether or not he was mentally cut out to play championship golf, if it in fact was his fate. The 1911 and 1912 U.S. Open Champion, John McDermott, had suffered a nervous breakdown just a few years earlier as the result of the stress of constant competition, and the thought had crossed

Jones's mind more than once that perhaps he might be cut from similar cloth. So it was not surprising that upon the eve of the U.S. Open at Inwood in 1923, Jones confided in his closest friend, O.B. Keeler, that if he didn't finally break through and win, it was a sign that it wasn't meant to be for him and that fate had other plans for his life.

What happened? Well, I don't think I'm exactly ruining the book for you to say that Jones did in fact break through and win that year and that a flood of both American and British titles followed in the next seven, culminating in the Grand Slam. I bring it up to highlight how close the player that was arguably the best to ever put on a pair of spikes came to quitting altogether after years of setbacks. Golf can be incredibly frustrating at times. I used to know a guy who often threw his clubs in the garbage can after a particularly frustrating round, only to retrieve them the following morning and pledge to begin anew. It became such a common occurrence that he forgot to retrieve them once, as he wasn't playing the next day, and the garbage truck actually picked them up, forcing him to purchase a new set before he could play again.

Each of us has his or her own challenges in the game, and there are certainly times when we all feel like dumping our clubs in the garbage, the lake, or the nearest gravel quarry, but real golfers rarely do. They say golf is like life, but in truth life is like golf. Inside every challenge there lies an opportunity, and while frustrating, there are a myriad of lessons to be learned from those less than perfect shots, holes, and rounds, as long as you pay attention and keep playing—even if they are just lessons in humility. Because the difference between a real golfer and one who no longer plays is no different than the difference between a champion golfer and a runner-up: perseverance. For as they say, the measure of a man is not whether or not he falls down, but whether he gets back up again. So *plan to persevere* and stay in the game, for you never know how close you are to success. It might be lurking around the next dogleg.

START AT THE FINISH LINE

"Focus on the process and the results will
take care of themselves."
– Dr. Stephen Simpson

One of the things that I am annually fascinated with is the culture of the New Year's resolution. Each and every year, a great many of us seem bound to embark upon a journey of some sort of self-betterment, and the dawn of a new year offers new hope for success on that ever-bumpy road. Now a great many of those resolutions will have something to do with working off those extra holiday inches that seem to annually accumulate around our mid-sections, but at least now and then many of us resolve to do something a little more lofty. We set our sights on some long-held goals (maybe even some that are golf-related) that we have had but have just never gotten around to doing anything about accomplishing.

While it now is a secular tradition, the concept of the New Year's resolution has many religious origins. The ancient Babylonians made promises to their gods each year to return any borrowed objects and repay old debts, while the Romans annually made promises to the god Janus, for whom the month of January is actually named. In medieval times knights took the "Peacock Vow" at the close of each Christmas season to reaffirm their commitments to the codes of chivalry. At Watchnight services many Christians prepare for the year ahead by praying and making new resolutions, and during Rosh Hashanah, Judaism's New Year, one is expected to reflect upon the past year's shortcomings with the intention of seeking and offering forgiveness. And while the Catholic practice of Lent and the annual sacrifices that come along with it take place in the weeks leading up to Easter, they are also at least partially responsible for the evolution of the current practice of New Year's resolutions.

The adoption of New Year's resolutions is growing in this country, too. At the end of the Great Depression, about a quarter of American adults admitted to making New Year's resolutions, while today that number has grown to over 40 percent. The problem, however, is despite their increase in acceptance culturally, along with that has come an acceptance of the fact that they seldom last and are often abandoned. A 2007 study by Richard Wiseman at the University of Bristol found that 88 percent of New Year's resolutions fail, despite the fact that 52 percent of the people in the study were confident of their success at the outset. Whether those resolutions are simply to get into better shape, to finally get your handicap down to single digits, or to attain some other lofty pursuit, the fact is that untold millions of Americans resolve each year to do something but unfortunately do it in a way that essentially sets them up for failure.

The first stumbling block is the nearly universal fact that commitments that we make to ourselves are generally the hardest ones to keep. Most of us get only four to six weeks into the New Year and our newfound resolutions when we trip up a few times and then give up until the next year. Despite those early bumps in the road, though, some of us will persist, vowing not to give up so easily but stumbling so often that, by May or June (maybe sooner), we are so far behind that we finally give up and decide to wait for the next new year and hit the reset button. The fact of the matter is it's not a new year that most of us need, but rather a new plan.

If you've been involved in business of any sort in the past couple of decades, you have likely heard of author Stephen Covey and his book *The 7 Habits of Highly Effective People*, where he coined the phrase, "Begin with the end in mind." While most of us can see the obvious wisdom in this statement and the idea of having an ultimate goal, it is a bit misleading because it only addresses half of the issue. Goal-setting does seem to help most men stick to their resolutions at a higher rate, but when it comes to women, peer support seems to offer a bigger advantage along the way. And while men and women alike set goals and often have support from their peers, the success rate in keeping resolutions is still abysmally low. This is in no small part due to the fact that it's all fine and dandy to know where you want to go and to have a few friends willing to join you and support you along the way, but you still need a roadmap of how to get there. So let me share with you a whole approach that I developed for my competitive players that I think will help you finally see some success.

As the wise Mr. Covey says, the first thing you need to do before you start any journey is to figure out where you're headed. If you're not sure what success ultimately looks like or exactly what you're shooting for, you will likely give up along the way. Open-ended decisions to do something without a finite goal to reach for or a predetermined destination will ultimately become pointless, and your work will become nothing but work for work's sake. Begin with the end in mind and decide what your goals are for the year, whether they be golf goals or otherwise. If your goals are golf-related, they might be things like lowering your handicap, increasing your distance off the tee, or qualifying to play in the scratch flight of the club championship.

These are performance goals, and they are the carrot, so to speak, but in order to accomplish them, you need what I call *process objectives* and short-term goals to help you get there.

These will be the foundation of your roadmap. So look at your performance goals and first break them down into measurable monthly goals that will be the reasonable intermediate steps along the way. If your goal is to get your handicap into single digits this year and you are currently sitting at 21, it is lofty indeed but at least easily measurable. Your monthly short-term goal will be to better your handicap by one stroke. Some analytics about your game (and likely some instruction) will be necessary to decide the best course of action, but for the sake of argument, let's just say that your pro tells you that you need to focus on improvement in all facets of your game equally to get where you want to go. This will require you to start keeping statistics, but knowing how many putts per round you make, fairways you hit, greens in regulation you hit, as well as a handful of other important stats will give you some great measuring sticks around which to craft your plan.

The next things you need to come up with are your process objectives. For golfers, I typically like to break these down into the following five categories: time management, nutrition and fitness, practice, mental game, and competition. Each individual can be a little different, but these areas are pretty universally important when building a roadmap to success for any golf-related goals. You and/or your pro will look at your long-term goal, settle in on the necessary short-term goals to accomplish it, then decide upon the necessary weekly process objectives you need to have built into your routine to help ensure you get there. I put time management first because it is very common to begin with a host of necessary objectives, only to stumble once you keep struggling to find the time to fit them all in. Humans are horrible estimators when it comes to project length, so you have to be realistic about the time you have to devote to your goal and build routines with your process objectives. They at first may seem overly conservative and slightly unambitious. Many a resolution has failed due to overcommitting to the point that success was near impossible to achieve.

The third thing you want to do to help ensure your success is to get some company. No matter what your goal is, you have a much better chance of achieving it if you have a buddy or two joining in the journey. If you're just picking up the game, maybe you've got another friend in the same boat who will want to take a regularly scheduled group lesson with you. If fitness is part of your process, find a workout partner, preferably one who doesn't make you feel like an out-of-shape wimp who hasn't seen the inside of gym since 12th grade P.E. class. If you're a driving range rat, look around; you've likely got plenty of company, as most clubs typically have an ample number of guys *and* gals daily beating their brains out, too. The key is to find that kindred spirit you can enjoy spending that time with, and it will make the whole process more enjoyable and keep you motivated. Even if you can't find suitable pals willing to join you on your quest (or at least help you along the way), make sure you make your goals public. Stating your goals to others, lots of others, repeatedly, really helps to keep you motivated. No one likes to be the one who's known for not following through, and knowing that you might be judged a little bit if you don't at least give your goals an honest effort will help keep you going during those moments when you feel like giving up.

Finally comes the most import part. While your short-term goals are monthly, you need to add one more little thing to your process that can serve as the tipping point to keep you going. At the end of each week, schedule a regular appointment with yourself to take a few minutes and analyze what went well that week and where you need to improve or make adjustments to your process. Then, during that appointment time at the end of each month, celebrate your accomplishments and start the whole process over. Don't carry anything over if you didn't accomplish it, just reset and begin anew with the next month's objectives and adjust your routine where necessary based on what worked and what didn't. The beauty of this is that no matter how badly you do one month, you can start over the next month. As long as your process objectives and your monthly short-term goals are in line with achieving your yearly goals, you will be excited to get back on track. You have to *start at the finish line* to know where you're headed, but once you do, your real focus should be on developing an organized and coherent process (your roadmap) to get there. That's why Dr. Simpson says, "Focus on the process and the results will take care of themselves."

PLAY FROM THE RIGHT SIDE

"The self-image is the key to human personality and human behavior. Change the self-image and you change the personality and the behavior."
– Maxwell Maltz

In the aftermath of Bubba Watson's amazing win at the Masters in 2012 and particularly in light of the true artistry of his winning shot, it was obvious to me that its real significance escaped both the media and the golfing public at large. While the shot—and Bubba's seemingly unique ability among his peers to execute it—were universally lauded, it is amazing to me that they haven't sparked a larger conversation about the lack of creativity, personality, individuality, and story amongst a majority of today's players on both the men's and ladies' tours. If the sport is going to survive, thrive, and grow back the audience and level of interest and participation that it had just a few short years ago, this should have been recognized for what it was: a proverbial Sputnik moment in the world of golf. We are at a moment in time where the industry at large needs to wake up and take a very hard look at itself and what it has become. And the fact that Bubba won the event twice in three years should only serve as further opportunity to reinforce this point.

Love him or hate him, Bubba Watson stands largely alone. With his homemade swing, go-for-broke style, Vesuvian personality, and seeming inability to hit two shots the same way, he is definitely a throwback to players of a bygone era. When you watch Bubba play, he reminds you more of Hagen, Palmer, Trevino, or Ballesteros than he does any of his contemporaries. He shapes shots left and right (as well as low and high) more than any other player on tour today and occasionally even seems to have fun doing it. And when you combine that with his prodigious length, sense of personal style, and even his penchant for putting his foot in his mouth now and again, you have a recipe for one of the more exciting and entertaining players of our day. With the modern golf ball and equipment having been continually engineered over the past 20 years to produce less spin and straighter flight, the ability to shape shots like players did only a couple of decades ago has been lessened considerably, which makes Bubba's ability (and seeming preference to do so) that much more remarkable. This technology shift has produced a generation of players who hit the ball longer and straighter than ever; however, it has simultaneously spawned an annual crop of players whose games lack a certain degree of creativity. As a result, we have far fewer players like Bubba or Seve, those whom you might call magicians, and in their place we have many more whom you might call Bob or Steve, who are more technicians.

The equipment isn't the only thing to blame, however. Tiger Woods and his nearly decade-long dominance of the sport inadvertently shaped the personality of this new generation of players, as well. Tiger's upbringing, obsessive work ethic, singular focus, stoic personality, and steely-eyed mental toughness were presented to us as the unquestionable blueprint for success in the modern era, and a generation of golfing parents were only too eager to buy in. Nike's marketing efforts, with their "I'm Tiger Woods" ad and the many that followed, were only too effective, the results of which we are just now starting to see—a tidal wave of players from around the globe that are, in a sense, little Tigers. If you likened their games and demeanors to other professions, it would not be too big of a stretch to call the majority of them accountants or managers—efficient, competent, and coldly effective, but largely devoid of personality. During this era, however, Bubba has somehow bucked the trend and emerged as an artist and an entertainer. He is an Indy car among a field of pace cars, who fittingly drives the General Lee from *The Dukes of Hazzard*. His ability to hit drives of jaw-dropping length (with a pink driver, no less) and to execute shots from areas most would call "no-man's land" seems not the slightest bit lessened by the fact that he often hits the head-scratching shots that leave him in those auspicious spots in the first place. Why, even his name is different. He takes obvious pride in the fact that his game can be accurately summed up by his personal mantra: "Give me a swing, and I've got a shot!"

I bring all of this up not as an exposé on Bubba or an attempt to politic for the position of president of his fan club. Nor does it come from the bias of a fellow lefty, for I would be just as happy to see Phil Mickelson or Mike Weir win the Masters again (well, maybe I am biased). I bring it up more as an examination of the state of today's game and to take a minute to examine why Bubba won (or at least a big part of the reason why) and why it was significant. While Bubba is obviously left-handed, he really plays the game from the right side ... the right side of his brain, that is.

The right side of the brain is responsible for all things creative and emotional, and if you saw the final hole and the aftermath on the green in 2012, these are areas of obvious abundance in Bubba. The left side of the brain is the residence of logic, reason, and analysis. It is the dominant side of the brain for all of those accountants, technicians, and managers and has been the side of the brain responsible for the information age and birth of calculators and computers. If you believe author Daniel Pink, who wrote *A Whole New Mind: Why Right-Brainers Will Rule the Future*, however, the era of left-brain dominance in our world has run its course, and the next few generations will belong to those who exercise and excel in skills and professions that demand right-brain thinking. The reasons for this are too numerous to go into, but for the sake of this book, let's just say that he is right and that the golf world must succumb to the same forces as do every other walk of life. This then means that they will need to embrace the changes that are already underway, and for whom Bubba's wins were just the nadir.

The landscape of golfers on TV for the past decade or so has been largely a mind-numbing army of robots—players for whom the word *imagination* is as foreign as the middle of the fairway is to Bubba. And whether or not the golf-consuming public realizes it, we crave creativity, personality, individuality, and story. We marveled at Tiger Woods and mostly cheered his dominance but never warmed up to him during that period of seeming infallibility in the same way that we did (and still do) for Phil Mickelson with his bewildered smile, amazing short game, and ever-present potential for a train wreck. And we still cheer for John Daly—maybe not as loud, but far more than we would for any other player with a similar record but less colorful persona. Some of the biggest draws at nearly every tour stop are names like Fowler, Poulter, Gulbis, and Creamer, players whose records arguably can't justify their gallery sizes but who exude personality.

Now for some, this may sound as if I'm saying that we crave style over substance, but that is an oversimplification. Bubba's popularity is in truth due to his ability to combine style with substance, but it is the style that puts him over the top. And Bubba's substance (as well as his Masters wins) in large part comes from his reliance on the right-brain skills of visualization, improvisation, and determination. While these are skills that might come more naturally to some than others, they can and should be both nurtured and developed. So now that six of the Masters winners since 2003 have been left-handed, I think we can safely say that Bubba's win signifies a shift not to but from the left (side of the brain, that is), and if golf is to experience a renaissance of sorts, more of his contemporaries should take a page from Bubba's book and embrace this shift.

And when it comes to your own game? Maybe it's time you learned to *play from the right side*—of your brain, that is—and begin a little work to change your self-image and the image you have of your game. You might start by improving your powers of visualization. Consciously try and shape shots more often and look for more creative and alternative routes every time you get into trouble. Play holes in different ways and with a different strategy than you might typically, laying up to a certain yardage or going for it once in a while if your nature is conservative. Maybe even update your wardrobe a bit, adding some bold colors, patterns, or a signature piece like a Hogan-style cap or even knickers. But even if you don't add new color to your wardrobe, the point is to find ways to add some new color to your game. You'll undoubtedly have more fun, and you might just find that you see the game from a whole new perspective.

Still not sure how to start? Maybe try hitting a few shots left-handed.

ACT LIKE YOU'VE BEEN THERE BEFORE

"Dreaming means rehearsing what you see, playing it over and over in your mind until it becomes as real to you as your life right now."
– Emmitt Smith

We've all seen it before. We're sitting around watching a professional sporting event when someone follows a fairly routine performance with an idiotic over-the-top celebration or fails to perform up to expectations and suffers a meltdown of epic proportions. It's the football player who makes a tackle and jumps up, rips off his helmet, beats his chest like Tarzan in his legendary call to the apes, and is subsequently flagged for a 15-yard unsportsmanlike conduct penalty. It's the basketball star who knocks down a three and struts back down the court hamming for the crowd, all while their opponent is blowing by them for a fast break on the other end. It's the tennis star protesting to the umpire about a ball that was clearly on the line, while slamming their $1,000 racket against the ground and swearing at the inept line judge who's obviously overdue for a trip to the optometrist. Or the golfer who misses a short putt, rushes the come-backer, misses it too, and then proceeds to toss his putter at his caddy, drop a few choice words for the spectators, and storm off to the scorer's tent, ignoring a line of kids asking for autographs on the way. We can't understand it—athletes at the highest level of their profession acting in ways that seem ridiculously inappropriate or as if they were completely unprepared for the situation they found themselves in. In a word, they act unprofessional. Could it be that in fact that before that moment in time they had actually never really been *there* before?

An ill-prepared brain can cause people to react in strange ways, particularly during times of stress, fear, and anxiety. Psychological studies performed by the military during World War II and backed up by numerous studies since then have found that, during times of extreme stress and fear, people's reactions predictably fall into one of three categories. Roughly 10-15 percent of people react appropriately and perform in ways necessary to accomplish what they need to. Another 10-15 percent of people basically freak out. They have a meltdown; they do something that seems completely inappropriate to the situation and for the most part go crazy. The other 70-80 percent? They freeze, which in the competitive sports world means *the moment* passes them by. They may not act out in ridiculous fashion, but they will go largely unnoticed because the moment itself essentially paralyzes them and causes either inaction or simply going through the motions. What is the key to acting like the top 10 percent? Preparation.

The British military has understood the importance of preparation for a while now and has studied it as it relates to combat so much so that they have come up with an adage for how they deal with it: the Seven Ps. *Proper Planning and Preparation Prevents Piss Poor Performance.* They put people through intense situation simulation for all of the potential realities that they may experience on the battlefield and as a result can much more accurately predict how soldiers will react during a given situation. This results in today's soldiers being among the most highly prepared in the history of warfare. This hasn't always been the case, however. The Brits were traditionally notorious for their stiff-upper-lip mentality, but studies after World War II found that over 70 percent of soldiers never even fired their weapon at the enemy, and during combat an extremely high percentage lost their lunches or worse. There is a reason today that we have inherited the term *shell-shocked*, and it has to do with the almost completely unresponsive state that many soldiers found themselves in after being subjected to the extreme stress of combat without being mentally prepared properly.

Now, it might seem a bit of a stretch to compare competitive golf and other sports to combat, and I am in no way trying to diminish what soldiers go through. I do so to highlight how being in a state of stress, anxiety, and fear (particularly for long periods of time) and how we have prepared for it can affect how we react during those moments. The parallels we see in the reactions of those competing at the highest levels of their profession are no surprise because in the brain's world, stress is stress, whether it is on the field of combat or the playing field. And one of the best methods we can employ in combating poor decision-making, freezing, or freaking out in those moments of truth is a sort of precision preparation that incorporates visualization. Most of us did a form of this quite naturally as kids. It was called *make-believe* and at the time it seemed the most natural route along the path to our dreams. Every putt was to win a U.S. Open, tee shots were our opening drive at the Masters, and approaches to the green were on the 18th of a major championship down one and needing a birdie. And while in retrospect this may have seemed like child's play, in fact this sort of rehearsal and situation simulation can be an invaluable tool during our preparation for competition. When you add to it new research that highlights how enhanced visualization techniques (incorporating actual successful images of what you are attempting to do) greatly increase your chances of success, you can begin to see what an invaluable tool these techniques can be when it comes time to act.

Now much of the research on the efficacy of enhanced visualization is fairly new, but the use of visualization has a long history in the game, and there evidence that some of the highest-level players have instinctively used it for years. Jack Nicklaus has famously claimed that prior to playing each shot he would see what amounted to a short movie of the swing he needed in his mind.

> "I never hit a shot, not even in practice, without having a very sharp, in-focus picture of it in my head," Nicklaus said. "First, I see the ball where I want it to finish, nice and white and sitting up high on the bright green grass. Then, the scene quickly changes, and I see the ball going there: its path, trajectory, and shape, even its behavior on landing. Then there is a sort of fade-out, and the next scene shows me making the kind of swing that will turn the previous images into reality."

And Nicklaus wasn't alone, but until the past decade or so, it was more commonly the domain of Olympic athletes. So while the golf world might have been a bit later to the party, it is finally beginning to gain wider acceptance. If you want evidence of this, you need only to have listened closely during the telecasts of Jordan Spieth's run at the modern Grand Slam in 2015. You would have heard his caddy repeatedly telling him to "get a good picture" prior to every shot, highlighting his practice of forming a clear mental picture of the shot he wanted to hit prior to hitting it. The additional use of images outside of our imagination, however, as a medium to aid and enhance visualization and learning is something whose positive effects are only now being more fully understood.

In recent research done at the University of Arizona by Dr. Debbie Crews, a video was created that showed putts of varying lengths and breaks being made over and over to a musical score. Researchers then took three groups of golfers and had them attempt a series of 10 putts for a pre-test, take a break, and then complete another series of 10 putts for a post-test. The first control group did nothing during the break and then reattempted the same 10 putts. The second group received a standard method of putting instruction along with verbal and visual cues during the break before reattempting the putts. The final group viewed a three-minute portion of the video of putts being made that had been created for the experiment. The results were pretty astounding. The control group improved 15 percent over their first attempts. The group that was given instruction improved 20 percent over their first attempts. The final group, the one watching the video, improved more than 60 percent over their previous attempts!

The success of this study really serves to highlight just how much potential the use of guided imagery can have, along with the aid of select images, when it comes to sports performance preparation. We have long understood the value of the images of those who are successful and have been successful at what we endeavor to do when it comes to perfecting the mechanics of a given motion, but this use of enhanced visualization shows how successful images can simultaneously serve as a stepping-off point in helping to develop mental images of things we wish to do, accomplishments we hope to make, as well as the physical motions we need to make to achieve them. Science is only just beginning to understand the purpose and power of mirror neurons in the brain, but in this instance we can cite their existence in order to put faith in how positive images can essentially help develop and enhance our powers of imagination and visualization, abilities which are increasingly being recognized as difference-makers when it comes to success in not only athletics, but music and other performing arts, as well. And the more vivid, detailed, and enhanced that visualization is, incorporating not just the mental and physical images, but the sounds, tastes, smells, and even the emotions we anticipate to be present, the more likely we will feel prepared for a given situation when it ultimately presents itself.

Muhammad Ali once said, "The man who has no imagination has no wings!" As more and more research on enhanced visualization and situation simulation unfolds, the more we begin to understand at least part of why men like Jack Nicklaus have flown so high. And as this understanding has begun to trickle down to the world of athletics, more and more high-level athletes and coaches are beginning to incorporate it into their training and practice regimens. Rehearsing potential scenarios over and over in your mind as you prepare for them (to the point where they almost do feel real) will at the very least make them seem far less foreign once we're actually in the moment. For most of us, however, we unfortunately abandoned the idea of playing make-believe as we got older, in much the same way we did so many other toys and pastimes of our youth. It came to be viewed as a mere manifestation of our immaturity, and in doing so we actually abandoned a very valuable tool of preparation. So the next time you find yourself in a stressful situation—on the golf course or otherwise—*act like you've been there before*. And if you haven't actually been there before, at least mentally, you shouldn't be at all surprised if your reactions aren't exactly what you'd have hoped for. Need a little help in getting there? Try YouTube. It's a veritable treasure trove of successful images and a great starting point in developing your own. See you on TV.

PART 7

ON FAITH, HOPE, AND

OPTIMISM

TAKE A QUANTUM LEAP OF FAITH

"Whether you think you can or think you can't,

either way you are right."

– Henry Ford

WARNING: The following is only a partial theory!

In medical science there is a common phenomenon known as the "placebo effect." It occurs when a treatment or medication without any proven therapeutic value is administered and a patient's symptoms improve. The patient believes and expects the treatment to work, so it does. In study after study, roughly 40 percent of people see improvement of their symptoms when administered a placebo, confounding the science of modern medicine. But while there remains inadequate explanation for the continual success of placebos from the field of medicine, at least one other field of science offers an explanation that at least in some arenas is starting to gain acceptance—physics.

There are times in life when our ultimate success requires a leap of faith. Believing in the unbelievable or that which is difficult or impossible to understand or prove is essentially the definition of faith. And deciding to walk down paths both questionable and unorthodox can simultaneously be a test of our faith and a testament to our desire to grow and succeed. I am aware, however, that faith aside, many of the related elements of the following subject are controversial. This is why it is not without some trepidation that I open the Pandora's box of quantum mechanics and a discussion of how it may or may not be a worthwhile topic in a forum devoted to the goal of improving your golf and your life. I do so, however, because you just never know if, for at least someone, this may be one of those aforementioned times.

I am a golf professional, not a physicist or metaphysicist, so let me be upfront by saying that I hold not much more than a layman's understanding of much of the following. But if you have been paying attention, by now you understand that if something holds just the potential to improve our odds of success in this game or in life, then I am inclined to give it closer inspection. While on the surface, the acceptance of the following premises might require more than a minor change in thinking, it has ever been my contention that in order to grow, get beyond old hurdles, and reach new heights it is sometimes necessary to open our minds to ideas we might instinctively dismiss.

Max Planck, Niels Bohr, Erwin Schrödinger, and Stephen Hawking aren't exactly household names when it comes to the world of competitive sports, but along with Albert Einstein, they advanced theories about subjects like general relativity, quantum mechanics, and string theory, which have led to hypotheses that can be argued to have, at the very least, an interconnected relationship with many elements required for growth and success in just about any field. While general relativity and quantum mechanics are only partial theories, which are as of yet irreconcilable (despite the unifying attempts of string theory), it is the theory of quantum mechanics that has likely led to the most debate of late. And this theory has simultaneously spawned further theories about concepts such as parallel realities, multiple dimensions, universal energy, the law of attraction, the law of cause and effect, along with a cottage industry of philosophical and self-help books, tapes, and programs whose claims could be considered dubious, fantastical, and potentially life-changing by turns.

I understand that string theory, general relativity, and quantum mechanics are among some of the most difficult concepts to wrap your arms around (not to mention explain in this short forum), and to some it might seem a bit of a stretch to relate them to the concept of playing a better game of golf. In truth, they might have absolutely nothing to do with improving your game, but there are some out there who feel they just might, so stick with me for a moment as I try to relate one way in which some performance coaches think they might potentially fit into the equation. And I promise to do it in as brief a manner as possible.

Quantum mechanics is the study of minute particles of matter and how they relate and interact with universal energy. The study of it and other similar subjects has revealed that the majority of what we perceive as solid matter is mostly just empty space. In fact, if you took all of the matter that makes up the entire population of everyone in the world, it would be smaller than a golf ball. The things we perceive to be solid, such as our clubs, balls, and selves, are really comprised of subatomic particles of matter and energy manifested into the objects that we see and feel. This is in part why unseen forces like gravity, radiation, radio waves, and cell phone signals can pass right through our bodies and other seemingly solid objects largely unaffected.

I realize this part is a bit of a recap, but as I mentioned previously, this unseen energy is all around us all of the time and it vibrates at a frequency that can be measured on an oscilloscope. The frequency and rate of vibration of the energy that makes up our bodies is apparently a function of our mood, attitude, and the qualities of character we most often display. A few years ago, one coach sent me a chart based upon these findings. At the bottom of the vibration range, you find emotions like fear, anger, anxiety, and depression, and you work your way up through progressively more benign ones until you reach confidence, wisdom, love, and gratitude at the top. As your mood moves up the chart from the negative to the more positive ones, the frequency and vibration rate of your energy increases, as well. The "law of attraction" theory claims that like energy attracts like energy and that, since you have the power to determine your mood and attitude, you subsequently should have the power to attract like people, circumstances, and events. When it comes to golf, this offers an explanation as to how your thinking may have an actual tangible effect upon your game. Dr. Stephen Simpson, a notable sports psychologist on the European PGA Tour, likes to say, "What you think comes out on the golf course," and if you accept the premise of these theories, it would seem that his mantra is pretty well in alignment.

Most golfers, at least occasionally, suffer from what another sports psychologist I know terms "stinkin' thinkin'." It could further be described as that little voice in their head that is constantly berating them after poor shots, telling them they're not good enough, and deriding them for not living up to their own perceived potential. And while they are often consciously aware that this type of negative thinking about themselves, their swings, or their game is counter-productive, the law of attraction, if accepted, could provide a deeper insight as to how insidious this type of thinking truly might be. And even if you don't buy into the supposed science behind it, these thought patterns are still self-limiting, and the longer you employ them, the more difficult they are to change, as they very often become habitual and, sadly, as comforting as an old blanket.

Albert Einstein, while most famous for his theory of relativity, is nearly as well recognized for his most attributable and aforementioned quote about the definition of insanity: "doing the same thing over and over and expecting a different result." This quote couldn't be more applicable when someone is struggling with some kind of personal growth. And golfers are no different, as those of us looking to grow our games most often need to change at least *something*—not necessarily our swing, brand of balls, or to the newest titanium-headed technology. We very often need to change how we think to grow our games, and to get started down that path we might just need to *take a quantum leap of faith* and open our minds to the possibility that if we learn to adopt the right mood and attitude towards our games (and just about everything else), it just might make getting where we want to go a whole lot easier. And like the placebo effect, it might not be necessary to understand how it all works (or to even be able to prove that it actually does), but rather to have an unwavering faith in the fact that, for reasons we are as of yet unable to adequately explain, it just does. Having faith in it may be a trip down the road less travelled, but sometimes that is the only road that will take us to where our lives, our work, and our games are finally in alignment with where we want to go. Best of luck along the way.

BECOME A SELF-FULFILLING PROPHECY

"Faith is to believe what you do not see;
the reward of faith is to see what you believe."
– St. Augustine of Hippo

If you were to look up *self-fulfilling prophecy* on Wikipedia, you would find it defined as a prediction that either directly or indirectly causes itself to come true, by the very terms of the prophecy itself, due to the positive feedback between belief and behavior. Similarly, we have what is known as the *Pygmalion effect*, named after the Greek myth of Pygmalion, a sculptor who fell in love with a statue he had carved. This phenomenon is based around the fact that the greater the expectation that is placed upon people, the better they generally perform. Both of these phenomena have one very important thing in common, without which they would and could not exist: faith.

Whether we are speaking specifically about self-fulfilling prophecies or the Pygmalion effect, people's beliefs seem to magically come true. This is largely due to the fact that they have complete faith in them and consequently are acting as if they are either already true or that failing is outside of the range of possibility. Rhonda Byrne disciples like to refer to this phenomenon as the aforementioned *law of attraction*, a term most recently popularized in her 2006 book *The Secret*, but the truth of the matter is, there is nothing very magical or secret about it. Our expectations change the way in which we behave, which in turn changes the way others behave towards us, thus reinforcing the conclusions of our original beliefs. Now, these beliefs can be either positive or negative, but it is obviously those of the positive sort that hold the potential to help us build confidence. And confidence is a big part of the faith in ourselves that is so critical along the road to success in golf or any other area of life.

So sticking with golf for the moment, there is another quote that I use quite often with students when we are working on developing strong mental game habits related to fulfilling their own little prophecies. It has been attributed to so many different sources that I'm not actually sure who first coined the phrase, but it is, "The body achieves what the mind believes."

This statement speaks to more than just the fact that confident golfers are more apt to achieve what they are attempting to do than those who lack confidence. When it comes to producing any type of golf swing (or any other motion, for that matter), having complete faith in your ability to do so is an invaluable asset. Part of this faith comes from the knowledge that you have the ability to perform the prescribed action and have done so previously, possibly many times even, but the second pillar of this faith comes from a quiet sense of confidence that you will be able to do so regardless of the circumstance or situation. In this instance past success sure helps, but true faith doesn't require actual proof to be present. I know this may sound a bit like a *chicken or the egg* line of logic, but stay with me a moment. In reality, there is a first time for everything, and if we don't develop at least a certain degree of faith in ourselves to succeed (even if we have never had success in or been in that situation before), it would be darn near impossible for anyone to ever accomplish anything.

So how do we develop that faith, particularly if our past history doesn't provide us with a lot of reason for believing in what we would like to see? New developments in neuroscience give a lot of credence to the age-old idea of *affirmations* being a big part of the secret. I understand that for a great many of you the concept of affirmations might bring to mind that old *Saturday Night Live* character Stuart Smalley and statements like, "I'm good enough, I'm smart enough, and doggone it, people like me!" But this stuff really works, and science is just now starting to figure out why. I won't bore you by going into all the gory details, but essentially our beliefs, the foundation of our faith, are nothing more than neurological pathways that are formed by what has been repeated over and over again, forming a pattern or "neuro-net." And as brain scientists are so fond of saying, brain cells that continually fire together wire together, which essentially means that after enough repetitions, our brains have trouble discerning between what is real and what is imagined. If we think about what we want to have happen enough and tell ourselves not only that it's going to happen, but that it's already a reality, we have the power to essentially create that reality, at least in our own minds.

Famous author and speaker Dr. Wayne Dyer is known for saying, "I'll see it when I believe it," which sounds an awful lot like what old St. Augustine was saying over 1,500 years ago. The truth of the matter is, though, that the concept of faith is timeless, and the power it can have in our lives transcends the ideas of any one person at any particular time. Believing in yourself and providing your brain with continual positive affirmations that back up that belief can go a long way to building an unshakeable faith that can ultimately have you seeing what you're believing. It doesn't matter if these habits of thought weren't your previous habits or how embedded the old patterns were, because the brain is malleable. With intention and enough repetition, you can literally rewire it to accept your new preferred beliefs. So as it turns out, I guess we can *become a self-fulfilling prophecy*. All we need to do is develop a little faith.

TAKE HEART AND HAVE HOPE

"All the great things are simple, and many can be expressed in a single word: freedom, justice, honor, duty, mercy, hope."
– Winston Churchill

I believe Winston Churchill to be not only one of the greatest men of the 20th century, but also the most quotable (outside of Yogi Berra). To include but one of his innumerable words of wisdom herein seems akin to recommending a Christian use but one passage in the Bible for daily guidance. Churchill's ability to consistently inspire, console, guide, and provide courage to the British people throughout the dark days of World War II is truly a book in and of itself (proven by the many that have been written), and I truly would never want to trivialize it by trying to draw parallels between those struggles and any struggles that we may have on the golf course. In golf and life, however, we all have our dark days, days in which we need a ray of hope to keep on fighting, and sometimes taking a look around at the struggles of others and what they have endured and overcome can be a great source of inspiration.

So with that thought in mind, I'd like to recommend you read Hank Haney's book *The Big Miss*, about Tiger Woods. While it is full of interesting revelations (especially for us golf instructors), I think the single most amazing thing I took away from it is that despite the prevailing notion for nearly two decades and all of the stories in magazines, on TV, on the Internet, and elsewhere, Tiger the golfer is in many ways not too different than the rest of us. It is a fascinating up-close look at one of the most dominant athletes of the past century, but regardless of his past dominance, it is simultaneously eye-opening how much Tiger dealt with (and still deals with) fears and insecurities about his game that nearly every golfer can relate to. And if you don't believe me, you only need point to his foibles around the greens in 2014 and 2015 for proof.

Hank's portrayal of this, a depiction somewhat akin to lifting back the curtain on the great and powerful Oz, is by some accounts blasphemous yet very human, and listening to Tiger's responses following its publication, I got the sense that this humanization, rather than any of the more tabloid-fodder material, is the thing that most bothered him about the book.

Tiger is and was an amazingly talented golfer, but he is also one who thrived and survived, for a very long time, on the fear and intimidation he seemed to perpetually strike into the heart of his opponents. He was the best front-runner ever, in large part due to the fact that when he was near to or possessed the lead going into Sunday, most of his competition appeared to accept the inevitability of his victories and seemed almost too eager to get out of his way. With very few exceptions (Bob May and Rocco Mediate come to mind), Tiger seemed to get out front and, as evidenced by his typically conservative Sunday strategy, wait for his competition to wilt. In the years since his last major victory at Torrey Pines in the 2008 U.S. Open, however, the concept of a Tiger victory being inevitable has become an almost quaint notion. Beginning not with his scandal, but with his loss to Y.E. Yang in the 2009 PGA Championship, his first loss in a major after holding the 54-hole lead, the sense of unwavering confidence Tiger seemed to eternally possess seemed to fade, and the near-universal belief in his mental dominance by other players slowly but steadily evaporated.

I write all of this not so much as a psychological treatise on Tiger or the state of his place in the game, but rather to highlight how even the best players deal with issues of fear, doubt, and insecurity. The title of Haney's book, *The Big Miss*, is, as much as anything, a reference to Tiger's fear of wildly hooking the ball off the tee with his driver (his big miss) and his seemingly never-ending quest for a swing whose mechanics would eliminate that fear. Tiger, now in the midst of his fourth major swing change after parting with instructor Sean Foley in 2014 and starting to work with Chris Como, disdains mental weakness and seems patently unable or unwilling to admit to it—not only to others, but also to himself. So not unlike a lot of us, he seems to cling desperately to the hope that perfecting his swing mechanics will cure most of his problems.

As golfers we've likely all heard before that the longest walk in game is from the driving range to the first tee, and listening to Hank, as well as witnessing Tiger's most recent struggles, this walk is obviously no shorter for one of the best players of the modern era than it is for the rest of us. His description of Tiger nearly always playing his home course at Isleworth in flawless fashion and going through the entire bag without missing a shot on the range before tournaments, only to step up to the first tee during an event and pop it up, block it straight right, or pull hook it into the woods is something that is so eerily familiar to most of us that it is almost astonishing. Now, as I've said before, I'm not saying swing mechanics aren't important, and it is definitely true that certain swings (especially those that rely heavily on the hands to square the club up in the hitting area) have more of a tendency to break down under pressure, but the obvious reality is that if you can hit it fine on the range and suddenly struggle on the course, then your problems are more mental than mechanical.

So for those of you who haven't yet read *The Big Miss*, I encourage you to pick up a copy, and I truly hope my little synopsis hasn't spoiled any of it. It's a good read, and the insight it provides on the struggles of one of our game's best ever can go a long way towards getting any golfer through some of those dark days. And for those of you who won't, I think I'll sum up its ultimate message (whether it was intended to be or not) as this: *take heart*, for you aren't nearly as far from greatness as you might think, *and have hope*, because the challenges and struggles that confront you every day are the very same challenges and struggles that have been met and bested by many of the greatest who have ever played. And that should undoubtedly provide everyone with inspiration.

BUILD UNCONDITIONAL CONFIDENCE

"Optimism is the faith that leads to achievement.
Nothing can be done without hope and confidence."
– Helen Keller

Long before the saying was popularized by the cult classic comedy film *The Adventures of Buckaroo Banzai Across the 8th Dimension*, Confucius was credited with saying, "No matter where you go, there you are." Similarly and more recently, I have heard it said that when it comes to most things in life, you can't ever really get anywhere other than where you started from. Figuring out how these complex concepts apply to playing better golf would require a long and winding trip down roads both philosophical and mystical in nature, but if you were to distill them down to their essence, you would find that, in relating them to confidence on the golf course, there are some very practical applications. To explain this, however, and to lay a foundation for their understanding that would really give you the keys to the kingdom, it is best to start by comparing it to the more familiar and approachable subject of happiness.

When it comes to happiness, the consensus opinion in the world of psychology is that most people fall into two camps: those who are inherently happy and those who seek/chase happiness (or who are inherently unhappy). Psychologists have long claimed that once someone is in possession of the basic necessities of life (food, shelter, and a modicum of security), happiness becomes a result of how one chooses to think. In the first camp, those who are inherently happy, circumstances have little effect upon how happy they are on a day-to-day basis. They take their happiness with them wherever they go, and it defines how they approach each obstacle and opportunity. In the second camp, those seeking/chasing happiness, you find the people for whom happiness in life is conditional. *They'll always be happy when...* When they get the new car, the new job, the new partner, the new house, the new whatever it is that they believe will make them happy.

The problem with those in the second camp and their worldview is that happiness that is based upon things outside of oneself is always short-lived because, by nature, it is conditional. They're happy when they get the new car, but after a little while, their focus shifts to the next thing they need to attain to keep them happy. It's a vicious cycle and the sort of mentality that is responsible for the actions of people like Bernie Madoff, the notorious Wall Street investment broker and ex-NASDAQ chief who, despite already being a multimillionaire, scammed people out of hundreds of millions of dollars in one of the most well publicized Ponzi schemes of this century. It's like trying to fill a glass with water that has no bottom. No matter how much you put in it, you can never fill it. And no matter how much you acquire, you can always get more, and therefore there is always something, someone, or some accomplishment to chase.

A state of happiness or unhappiness is essentially a choice that you make; however, a great majority of us have become so habitually inclined to make the same particular choice that we are mostly unaware that we are doing so. Whether you are happy or unhappy is very truly a decision you make about how you will experience each moment. They are two different pairs of glasses through which you chose to see the world, that transcend the mere concept of the optimist or the pessimist. So when it comes to true happiness, it is not a place that you get to—you either are or you aren't already there.

Confidence works in much the same way, and it would not be too far a stretch to say that among all the qualities necessary to get your golf game to the next level, confidence is the most critical. Just as in the happiness example, a great majority of golfers practice conditional confidence. *They'll be confident when...* When they start to make a few putts, after they hit a few good tee shots, once they post a couple of good rounds, or once their swing is where they need it to be. Can you now see the problem with this? Sure, having some success can provide a short-term jolt of confidence that may see you play well for a brief period of time, but if your confidence is dependent upon these occasional successes, I have some bad news for you. You are essentially golf's version of Bernie Madoff.

Golf is a game in which you will experience far more failures than successes, and if you are choosing only to be confident once you achieve success, you are putting the cart before the horse and will rarely play any part of any round where you truly feel positive about your game. If optimism is the faith that leads to achievement, then you need to decide in advance that you will have confidence, despite whether or not you believe you've acquired any reason to be. You can't wait for the planets to all line up or the putts to all start rolling in before you're willing to be confident. And if by chance you've been waiting to be confident until you think your swing is perfected, that might be the biggest fool's quest of all. Even Ben Hogan, one of the most prolific ball-strikers of all time, claimed that he only hit four or five shots a round exactly the way he wanted to—and he was Ben Hogan.

So hopefully, you now have a little better understanding of why I said that you can't get anywhere other than where you started, so make the decision to be confident in your ability regardless of results, or you will be forever chasing. Be confident in your ability to hit it straight and true from the tee, because whether it was on the course or the range, you've done it hundreds and likely thousands of times before. Be confident in your ability to get up and down after missing that green, because you've done that, too, and those prior successes weren't flukes, but rather what happens when you finally get out of your own way. And be confident the next time you step up to that three-foot putt for par or birdie, because you know what? When you really think about it, we've all made thousands more of those three-footers than we've ever missed, and even for the poorest of putters, the odds are ultimately in your favor. And if you miss, that's O.K., too, because once you decide to *build unconditional confidence*, you won't have trouble keeping that miss in perspective and remembering that, ultimately, no matter where you go, there you are.

TAKE CHARGE OF YOUR OWN GAME

"You must take personal responsibility. You cannot change the circumstances, the seasons, or the wind, but you can change yourself. That is something you have charge of."
– Jim Rohn

When it comes to the idea of becoming a better golfer, I really believe that most golfers on the whole are fairly optimistic about their prospects. Sure, everyone has their dark moments, days, or rounds when it seems possible that we could even shank our putts, but the widespread popularity of the saying, "That's the kind of shot that keeps you coming back!" following the one or two nice shots most of us hit during a round speaks to the inherent optimist deeply embedded somewhere in us all. So while we all tend to hope and sometimes even pray to find a way to unleash the better golfer that we instinctively know is inside of us, the ways in which we endeavor to unchain that better golfer can often take two terribly divergent paths. And while each party believes in the efficacy of their route and is optimistic about their chances, their experience as a whole, rate of improvement, and ultimate success can often look very different depending upon which they chose. Let's take a look at each party and the path they are most likely to take.

The first party of golfers we will call the Democrats. I know, I can already hear you crying, "Hasn't the media stereotyped us enough already?" or, "Don't go trying to bring politics into this discussion!" But stick with me a moment, as while the monikers are fairly tongue-in-cheek, they are simultaneously apropos. We all know golfing Democrats. They are the ones staking themselves to every tree the Greens Committee has decided to remove, calling for a moratorium on golf carts and a return to walking as they do in Europe (for everything done in Europe is better), and the board member at the club annually clamoring for a dues increase. They believe in fixing your ball mark and one other, the leveling of the playing field provided by handicaps, and the availability of free tees in the golf shop; they are the ones who think the club pro should be walking the range tee each morning passing out free tips. Yes, the golfing Democrat wants and is not afraid to ask for a little help. It might be on the range, from a playing partner, or even the club professional from time to time, because when it comes to improving their golf games, he or she is more comfortable when the responsibility for that prospect lies in someone else's hands. The Democrats profess to want to improve their games as much as the next guy but secretly crave the ability to abdicate the responsibility for that improvement in case things don't work out.

The second party is, of course, known as the Republicans—aaah, the party of personal responsibility. We've all got at least a Republican or two in our regular foursomes. They're the ones who always want to play straight up, who believe everyone *else* is a sandbagger, and whom you have to fight tooth and nail before they're willing to give up even a single stroke. They prefer stroke play or match, as long as it's individual, and disdain scrambles and best balls since they are the domains of the golfing weak. They decry the club's inability to run like a business, incessantly complain about divots and everyone else's inability to fix them, all the while driving their street legal souped-up golf carts with the stereo blasting just about anywhere and anytime they please. When it comes to their games, they want to get better, too, but they're not looking for a handout, preferring to self-manage, as they don't really like being dependent upon someone else. Their do-it-yourself approach often leads to solitary hours spent on the range, beating balls until their hands bleed, in a desperate attempt to find something, anything that will work and leave them with that self-satisfied sense of pride for having figured out how to do it on their own.

Now, obviously these are both a bit facetious, but they can and do go at least a little way towards explaining why you may inherently prefer one learning style over another. There are, however, often elements of both personality types in every golfer, so don't be alarmed if any of you self-professed elephants out there found at least a little bit of yourself in the description of our friends, the donkeys. You see, whether you're a Democrat or a Republican, it is funny how, while both parties are eager to improve their games, we often find that a great majority of people (at least initially) are reticent to ask for help. The popularity of *Golf Digest*, *Golf Magazine*, and the Golf Channel instruction programs are a testament to this preference many golfers have for the go-it-alone approach, and as a result, those who eventually do come to us professionals for lessons often come armed with such an arsenal of preconceived notions about what they are doing right or wrong and what they need to do to improve that they have become as unreceptive as the Buddhist's proverbial upside-down cup.

When anyone is convinced that they already know something, they will tend to speak or listen only through their own preconceptions and often stop listening in order to strenuously protect the point of view they are invested in. Recent studies done of brain activity may actually shed some light on why this is the case. Apparently, when one is receiving advice, the part of the brain that lights up is the same region that is associated with pain, and when giving advice, the part that lights up is that which is associated with pleasure. For us parents, this could also explain why our kids never seem to be willing to take our advice on merit and must inevitably end up learning everything the hard way. It's actually painful for them to hear it! When it comes to golf, however, this reticence to ask for help can be a big roadblock on our journey to self-improvement, and it doesn't have to be that way.

There is a saying that I heard a few years back and that I believe is finally gaining a little traction in the golf instruction world: "Golf cannot be taught and really must be learned." For some of us who have made a living teaching, it is a breath of fresh air, because while we teach members of both parties, it seems we are beset by a much larger percentage of Republicans! For these folks and their desire to take responsibility for their improvement, learning golf can be accelerated if they can find the right coach who understands their personality, capabilities, unique learning style, and preference for a certain degree of independence. Armed with that information and an understanding of how best to teach and communicate to a student an awareness of what is happening in their own swing, the most effective path for a great many of these students is to foster their ability to self-coach. And at least for members of that party, it is a path to improvement that shows far more promise than the traditional student/teacher dynamic that has been the sole model for golf instruction up until fairly recently.

After all, the solitary ball-beaters we see daily out on the range are living testament to the fact that, for many of us, being able to figure it out for ourselves is much more pleasurable than surrendering all of that responsibility to someone else. That's why if you want to remain optimistic about the prospects for improvement, it might just be time to *take charge of your own game* and learn a little more about the idea of self-coaching. Not only will your brain likely enjoy the experience more than listening to the advice of a typical golf instructor, but you might even figure out for whom you should be voting in the next election.

FOCUS ON YOUR GOOD SHOTS

"Better to keep yourself clean and bright, for you are the window through which you must see the world."
– George Bernard Shaw

In over 25 years of teaching golf, I have yet to have a student turn to me after a good shot and say, "What did I do right there?" Conversely, just about every top, skull, chunk, shank, flub, hook, or slice I have ever had the misfortune of witnessing has been almost immediately and reflexively followed by a student's plea of, "What did I do wrong?" At times it seems that the game breeds pessimism (or at least inherently attracts more than its fair share of pessimists), and as golfers we seem to almost instinctively focus on the negative (or the thing that we'd rather *not* happen) than what we wish would come to pass. We look at each hole and see the bunkers, the hazards, or the ever-narrowing hallway of trees that line each side of the fairway we are hopelessly attempting to play to. We look at our shots with disdain when they go even slightly awry and seem almost embarrassed to congratulate ourselves too much when they are good. We seem to want to make sure everyone (including ourselves) knows that we've "been there, done that" and we naturally expect to do it again.

By contrast, when I watch football these days, it seems the majority of players are jumping around, chest bumping, and celebrating after even the most routine of plays. Football players, at least, seem to be really focused when they do something right and aren't afraid to let the whole world know that they have. In golf terms, this would be somewhat akin to Tiger Woods celebrating every made two-footer for par with his signature fist pump (although given his most recent play, maybe he should). We golfers are a different breed, though, and keeping our composure and displaying proper etiquette are grilled into us at an early age. But is there by chance a little something we can take from the habits of those on the gridiron that would apply to our 7-irons? Now, I'm not recommending you start strutting around and shouting "You da man!" every time you hit a green in regulation, but I am suggesting that there is a great deal of overlooked value in a little exultation now and then and a lot of internal focus upon those moments of success. Let's start with the practice tee.

As I mentioned previously, we can tend to stand out on the range, beating ball after ball, giving scant attention to those shots that go in our intended direction, while overly analyzing every less than successful effort. The next time you're out there, try doing exactly the opposite. Immediately discard each poor shot, both physically and mentally, by raking another ball and at least mentally waving them off as you would an annoying mosquito. For those good shots, however, try first giving yourself a little mental pat on the back after each one, and follow that up with a short period of reflection about what you were thinking of just prior to and during the execution of the swing. Were you thinking of a rhythm cue, visualizing the shot, or maybe even humming a few bars of your favorite tune? Did you have a picture of the target in your mind's eye, a particular swing thought rattling around in your head, or was everything pleasantly, almost abnormally quiet? Do this exercise often enough, and you will usually start to notice similar elements and patterns of thought leading up to and during the swings of the shots that were successful. These are the things you want to start focusing on to consciously develop a routine.

Now let's take a look at a little tool I like to use for players once they get ready to head out to the course. This one will require a little homework, but the time spent focusing on it will be time well spent. Most golfers that have played for any length of time have hit plenty of successful, even great golf shots. If you take a moment, it is likely you can recall at least a good shot or two with even the clubs that you struggle with the most. Get a pen or pencil and a pad of paper and write down every club in your bag on the left hand side. To the right of that, write down the best shot you can ever remember hitting with that particular club or a shot you made with that club in a particularly stressful or pressure-packed situation. If you striped a driver off the first tee during the horse race of the Men's Invitational with 200 people watching last year, put that shot down as your best shot for your driver. If you hit a perfect 7-iron on that tough par three over water at your home course that took two bounces, skidded to a stop, and trickled in for a hole-in-one five years ago, put that down next to your 7-iron. If you made a seven-foot side-hill breaker to win a $2 Nassau over one of your best golfing buddies recently, put that down next to your putter. Do this until you have a good shot that you made at some point with every club in the bag or in every situation.

Now that you essentially have a diary of your best shots to draw from, go through the bag (mentally) and visualize each of these shots over and over again while attempting to recreate and relive the emotions you felt upon hitting them. Once you have done that repeatedly, you will be in a position to trigger those memories each and every time you pull that club out of the bag to hit a shot. Use these memories to set the stage every time you are standing behind the ball and visualizing the shot that you plan to hit next with that club. This type of continual positive focus, if given repeated attention, will eventually develop into a habit that you instinctively perform upon going into your routine. I know it's not easy at first to stop obsessing over all those chunks, tops, and skulls and to give up on the type of thinking that this will help you to avoid them in the future. It may be even harder to give yourself that little mental pat on the back when you do succeed, but if your mental outlook truly is the window through which you look upon the world, then developing the habit of *focusing on your good shots* will ensure that at least your window will be clean and free of the mental dirt that keeps most of us from succeeding. Time for some Windex?

PART 8

ON HONOR, TRUST,

AND CONVICTION

A GAME OF HONOR

"A nation reveals itself not only by the men
it produces, but also by the men it honors,
the men it remembers."
– John Fitzgerald Kennedy

The game of golf has been called a game of honor. It is the only game in which you call penalties on yourself, so I guess it is not surprising that this game has produced sportsmen and women of incredible distinction over the years and that it rightly continues to honor them to this very day. Too often in the modern sports world, we hear that our most distinguished athletes shouldn't be held up as role models—and for good reason, for too often today's media (the same media that seems to be in such a hurry to build up these athletes to the point of being icons) seems just as eager to tear them down from the pedestal upon which they have been placed. And unfortunately, our modern sports athletes give them ample reason to do so far too often.

Obviously, there are as many reasons for this as there are different situations, and I am not here to debate the problems and pressures faced by today's men and women athletes. What I would rather do is pose a question. Wouldn't it be nice if there were at least one sport where these unfortunate situations were the exception rather than the norm? A sport that regularly produced men and women of character who truly appreciated the opportunity to be an ambassador for it and to honor it by their example? A sport whose true significance was revealed by the fact that it always gave more than it took, not only to those who played it, but to multitudes who can't even claim any real association with it? Well, this is the unique space in which I believe the game of golf historically resides, and it is where I feel it continues to distinguish itself from all other sports that are played at both the amateur and professional level.

From Bobby Jones and Alexa Stirling to Ben Hogan and Jack Nicklaus, the game has left us a legacy of men and women who were not only great players, but also great citizens and role models who embodied the truest examples of sportsmanship while giving back to the game, their communities, and their country. Bobby Jones, long before his historic Grand Slam, paired with his childhood friends Alexa Stirling (winner of three straight U.S. Women's Amateur Championships) and Perry Adair to form the "Dixie Kids," a famed group of phenomenal young players who travelled around the country during World War I playing exhibitions to raise money for the Red Cross. During World War II, many golfers famously enlisted into the various armed services, including Jones, Ben Hogan, Horton Smith, Porky Oliver, Sam Snead, and Jim Turnesa. Two that earned distinguished service were Lloyd Mangrum (two Purple Hearts), and former U.S. Open champion Jack Fleck, who participated in the D-Day invasion at Utah Beach. Considering that, I guess it's no small wonder he wasn't too intimidated by the more accomplished Hogan in that famous playoff at The Olympic Club in 1955.

Speaking of Hogan, while his service in the U.S. Army Air Forces was notable and his playing accomplishments speak for themselves, it is a more little known fact that might distinguish him beyond his on-course achievements. In 1948, early one morning on a fog-shrouded bridge, Hogan and his wife Valerie were in a head-on collision with a Greyhound Bus. The only reason Hogan survived and went on to face Fleck and many others afterwards was the fact that he threw himself across his wife Valerie to protect her and subsequently avoided being impaled by the steering column, which was driven through the driver's seat. And Nicklaus, while revered as the man who still holds the record for the most major championships ever, might also hold the record for the single greatest act of sportsmanship ever recorded. It took place during the final hole of the final match of the 1969 Ryder Cup. After making a five-foot putt for par, Nicklaus conceded a three-and-a-half-foot putt to Tony

Jacklin to halve the hole and halve the Ryder Cup matches. Nicklaus is undoubtedly one of the greatest competitors of all time, but not so competitive that he couldn't make a magnanimous gesture that might have spared a fellow competitor from the ultimate embarrassment. Can you imagine anything similar happening in any other sport anywhere?

Now, I could go on, but I want to assure you that I'm not a total Pollyanna for the players of yesteryear and that there are plenty of examples of why the game's contributions (and contributions to the game) didn't die with our country's greatest generation. The game of golf currently raises more money for charity than all other professional sports combined. Every player on the Men's, Ladies', and Senior Tours gives of their time weekly to participate in events that generate money for charities of every conceivable type, and many have their own foundations that raise money for various causes around the globe. The First Tee teaches life skills while introducing the game to millions of kids around the country who might otherwise never be touched by it. And through the game, you likely have contributed in numerous ways yourself. One of those ways is through an organization known as the Folds of Honor Foundation, which was founded by Major Dan Rooney, a PGA professional and former F-16 pilot in the Oklahoma Air National Guard. This organization has raised money to help provide scholarships for over 2,000 recipients whose parents or spouses have been killed or injured in the line of duty serving our nation. A great many clubs around the country have participated in their annual national fundraiser in various ways, but the most common is by donating a dollar of your greens fee for every round played over the Labor Day weekend.

So the next time you are thinking about your involvement with the game and how much space and time you dedicate to it, remember some of the less obvious benefits to making and keeping it an important part of your life. It is an honorable game that builds and reveals character. It is a game that gives back and a game without which I'm sure we would all feel as if something were missing. And if you have a friend, a child, or a grandchild who seems to be missing something in their lives, why not consider introducing him or her to this *game of honor*? It may seem like a small thing in contrast to the contributions that some of the greats have made, but in reality, in what better way could we really honor this game?

A CALL TO IRONS

"Infinite striving to be the best is man's duty; it is its own reward. Everything else is in God's hands."
– Mahatma Gandhi

Once upon a time, being known as the best player at any respective golf club was an honor that carried a little more reverence than it does at many clubs today. "The Club Championship" was almost universally regarded as the most important event of the year, and being the "Club Champion" was a position of some distinction. For a great many golfers, the annual quest to become their club's champion was something to plan one's year around, as many relished the opportunity to test his or her mettle and measure their improvement against the club's elite players. It is not a coincidence that most amateur golf information guides still list each club's men's and ladies' champions in their directory each year, and it is still common practice for most clubs to hold their championships well into the golf season, giving potential competitors ample opportunity to practice and allow their games to round into form in anticipation. At some point, however, there began a slow but steady erosion of this long-standing tradition, and "The Club Championship" lost its place as each club's preeminent tournament to events like invitationals or qualifiers in which players of varied ability could team up and take a shot at advancing to a competition beyond their respective clubs. To begin to solve the riddle as to when and why this took place, I believe a little history is in order.

The Scots are historically given credit for inventing the game of golf. A lesser-known fact, though, is that they also likely invented the precursor to the modern handicap system. "Assigning the odds" is what the Scots referred to the practice of handicapping as, and the "adjustor of the odds" was he who most closely resembled our modern-day handicap chairman. Their earliest attempts at handicapping golf events, however, didn't benefit the competitors, but rather the bettors. As a result, the Scots, and their nearly insatiable appetite for a wager, unknowingly created a monster! Even more so than today, it was not uncommon at that time for there to be two or three golfers of exceeding ability playing in each club's tournament, but the Scots endeavored to bring more horses into the field, and handicapping the competitors increased the number of individuals that one might bet upon and subsequently increased the total of bettors and money in the betting pools. The natural progression of this, of course, was the idea of conducting tournaments where players would be given a certain "allowance" of strokes in order to compete against players of greater or lesser ability. All this aside, however, even taking into consideration the rise of a unified handicap system in England during the late 1800s, the club tournament (played at scratch)—or club championship, as it is more commonly called today—remained the preeminent annual event at most golf clubs around the world until the latter half of the 20th century.

So why and at what point did being the best golfer at any given club become something that fewer and fewer golfers annually desired to strive for? Could it have been a classic Communist plot? The handicap system does bear some resemblance in principle to something Karl Marx might have devised, but the Scots have little historical involvement with Communism, and considering the "red scare" of the 1950s in this country, I am quite certain that a former Senator McCarthy and the House Un-American Activities Committee would have likely uncovered it long ago if there were any dubious connections. Have instructors and equipment manufacturers failed to help the masses? Well, vast improvements in equipment have left little excuse for the average player not to be able to get clubs that fit properly and make the game easier, and quality golf instruction has never been more available, so I believe those are the least likely reasons that we have seemingly settled into a comfort zone of mediocrity. Is it the sandbaggers? Sure, at one point or another, we've all become tired of losing to those who have managed to acquire an "allowance" of strokes that seemingly exceeds their ability, but so much so that we have en masse adopted an "if you can't beat 'em, join 'em" mentality? Well, I hope not, so in place of all these theories, let me at least offer one other.

The game of golf in and of itself is not always fair. Just like life, there are bad bounces and breaks that we all suffer, and there are those that can make this difficult game look incredibly easy. The goal of the handicap system was and is to facilitate fair competition amongst players of every ability. Inadvertently, however, this leveling of the playing field (and the opportunity it allows for players of every ability to enter the winner's circle) may have robbed some of their incentive to improve. Most club champions work hard on their games, play to scratch, and are consequently some of the finest amateur players in their respective areas. They typically compete beyond the local level, often testing their mettle in high-profile amateur events against other players of similar abilities and on other courses. Despite all this, how many of you out there reading this would even recognize your club's own champion if he or she were hitting balls next to you on the driving range? Better yet, how many of you are honing your skills as we speak so that you will be ready to answer the bell when it comes time to challenge him or her this year in *your* club's championship? Anyone?

So this is my call to arms (or irons, if I may). It's time to dust off those woods, file those wedges, renew your commitment to the game, and head to that lonely place called the practice tee. If you need directions, check with your local **PGA** professional. If you seem to have forgotten how to use those clubs, I'm sure he or she will be more than willing to help with that, too. Because while being the next club champion might not realistically be on everyone's radar this year, we can each establish our own goals and in the process go back to a time when we used our handicap as more of a measuring stick of our improvement, rather than a convenient excuse for not seeking to. See you on the practice tee...

MISS IT, NOONAN!

"It's good sportsmanship not to pick up lost golf balls
while they are still rolling."
– Mark Twain

Watching professional golf the past half-dozen years, the overarching storyline has been the struggles both on and off the course of Tiger Woods. While early on, the focus was more on his off-course troubles, in the past few years, the spotlight has shifted more to his struggle to regain his form. And if you listen to all the pundits and prognosticators in the golf world, they seem to have made one fairly consistent observation. Tiger Woods, while seemingly in a better place mentally after getting his personal life in order, just isn't the same player he used to be. The reasons and opinions as to why are typically chalked up to a combination of factors, including age, injury, poor putting, inferior (to earlier incarnations) swing mechanics, and a loss of confidence and the sizeable mental edge he used to possess over other players. There is one factor, however, that I have yet to hear discussed in any way that could potentially be the biggest obstacle Tiger now faces in his effort to regain his form and begin anew his assault on Jack Nicklaus' record of major championships. What is that obstacle??? You!

Over the past three decades, Princeton University's School of Engineering and Applied Science has conducted a program called PEAR, which is short for the Princeton Engineering Anomalies Research Program. The scientist who began this undertaking did it originally in an attempt to disprove Einstein's theory that the intent of the scientist influences the outcome of the experiment, but after 30 years, their overwhelming conclusion was that Einstein was right.

The most substantial portion of the PEAR program examined anomalies arising from human/machine interactions, with the study tracking how focused human intention affected outcomes of random number generators. They performed thousands of experiments where people were essentially asked to focus their intent on the number *one* to see if they could influence the devices to produce more *ones* than *zeroes*. Again and again, the research showed that people's intent skewed the results of the machines, even if they were unaware of the presence of the machine or the intent of the experiment. In addition to that, the more people who were involved in the experiment at the time, the greater the degree to which the outcomes were skewed.

The next logical step in demonstrating the effects of human consciousness on physical realities was to test it on people. They had people sit in one room and asked them to randomly draw shapes or numbers on a piece of paper, while, unbeknownst to them, people in another room were thinking of a specific shape or number. Again and again, the people drawing the shapes or numbers drew a disproportionately greater number of the shapes or numbers which the people in the other room were thinking of, proving the effect of people's focused intent on others. This even proved to be true when the subjects were thousands of miles apart. This is an astonishing discovery, the effects of which we are only beginning to understand, so if you are interested in reading more about it, you can do so at princeton.edu/~pear.

Now when it comes to the realm of professional sports, this research, if nothing else, proves that the home field advantage is not just an intangible edge, but also a physical reality. Imagine going into an arena where there are thousands of people whose focused intent is on your failure. Not only is it loud, intimidating, and disruptive, but there is an obvious unseen psychic force at work, as well, that has you swimming against the tide of focused human intent.

Golf is the most mental sport there is, and for Tiger Woods, it has ever been a given that he has a mental edge over his opponents, but that was mostly during a time when the predominant number of people in any gallery, in any tournament, and in the golfing world were rooting for Tiger. Could it be that his mental edge was at least partially due to factors outside of himself? Since Tiger's well-documented fall from grace a few years ago, the number of Tiger supporters out there has plummeted. For the past few years, Tiger has had to deal with the fact that there are often more people rooting against him than there are rooting for him, and to a certain degree, it shows. His post-round press conferences are short or non-existent and his answers terse, often showing a disdain for those asking the questions and a level of impatience with them previously unseen. Sure, Tiger was never a prince when it came to the media, but the focus of so many disapproving eyes has too often turned that million-dollar smile into a glare and a scowl.

Now I want to give credit where credit is due, because Tiger has at times (when he isn't injured) looked somewhat like the Tiger of old, but he hasn't won an event of any real significance since the 2008 U.S. Open. And when he has had the opportunities, unlike the Tiger of old, time and again he seems to falter when the spotlight is brightest, the stakes are highest, and the focused intent of the golfing world is most squarely on him. In a game where intangible elements like confidence can be the difference between a missed or made five-footer to save par on a Sunday, having the (psychic) wind at your back (rather than in your face) might just be the difference between rolling it into the heart and pulling it just a hair, causing it to lip out, or roll just by. And the difference in Tiger's level of confidence, whether it be standing on the tee with his driver on a tight par four, chipping from around the greens with a tight lie, or standing over an important five-footer for one of those par saves he once made so routinely, might be at least partially due to the fact that more people are hoping he misses it than the other way around. It brings to mind that legendary scene from *Caddyshack*, when poor Danny Noonan was trying to make that critical final putt to win the caddy tournament, while the majority of the onlookers were shouting, "Miss it, Noonan!" And while Noonan made that last putt anyway, this isn't Hollywood, and at least for the present, if more people don't start rooting for Tiger again, we can't be sure if his true-life story will play out for him with a similar happy ending.

GIVE UP CONTROL TO GET CONTROL

"The person most in control is the person
who can give up control."
– Frederick S. Perls

If you've played golf for any length of time, you've undoubtedly heard someone, even possibly yourself, mutter something like, "Steer job," "Tried to guide it," or "Held on to it!" after a bad tee shot that ended up in the trees, the bunker, or worse. I call these frustrations *phraselets* (I know it's not a word), but they are really our way of saying that we tried to exert too much control over our swing, rather than just letting go and swinging free. It's a very common problem in the game that we've likely all experienced at one time or another and one for which even the "Klingon death grip" on the club is an unsuccessful antidote. It can arise for various reasons in various people, but the personality types most typically afflicted tend to be perfectionists, control freaks, and those individuals whose oversized ego has left them too attached to a specific outcome and unable to accept the consequences of failure to perform up to the level of ability they truly (or at least wish to) possess.

This breakdown in our abilities due to attempting to exert too much control isn't just limited to golfers, though. Pay close attention and you will see it in just about every type of sport when a player is given a little too much time to think. It is the basketball player who is a great shooter but who suddenly has trouble with free throws. It is the second baseman who fields a routine ground ball and throws it in the dirt or over the head of the first baseman. It is the tennis star who suddenly is hit with a rash of double faults who has heretofore been a great server of the ball. The better we get at any given athletic endeavor, the more of a tendency we have to try to over-control the motion and mechanics of what we are attempting to do, and at least some of that comes from an acute awareness of our ability to do just that. Unfortunately, though—and especially during those moments when the chips are down and the stakes are highest—our desire to exert that control often coincides with the moments when we most need to trust in our natural abilities and just perform.

When we try to control our golf shots too much, we are playing with our conscious mind, which is rarely a good ingredient when you're trying to play your best golf. We try to control things because of what we think may happen if we don't, which essentially means our desire for control is rooted in fear. Our best golf is played with the subconscious or intuitive mind, but it is difficult to access those abilities when we are afraid and thus trying to exert too much control. The subconscious mind knows how to swing the golf club, just as we know how to walk, chew gum, and carry on a conversation at the same time. We don't have to tell our legs to move one foot in front of the other to get where we are going, we just walk and we walk a pretty straight line. It is something we know how to do, and there is neither consequence nor payoff for walking that straight line, so it is easy. Now put us on a two-foot wide beam several stories up, and suddenly we start thinking about the mechanics of walking. It's not any more difficult; it's just that the consequences of our success have changed dramatically, so we are much more attached to a particular outcome.

The actual process of learning to give up control can be very different for everyone, depending upon which aspect of your life you most need to do so. In most situations, however, a likely first step is to let go of your ego. When it comes to golf, who are you really trying to impress anyway and who's going to care what you shot (other than you) by tomorrow? A common next step is to stop being such a perfectionist and expecting perfect outcomes. So much unnecessary stress is derived from a desire for perfection. Besides, when it comes to golf, don't we all admire that scrappy player who forever seems to be making lemons into lemonade anyway? Another potential step is to take a step back and stop needing to be in charge of everything. Let your spouse pick the restaurant you go to for dinner, let your coworker or employee head up the next project, or let your playing partner drive the cart for once. If you're an over-planner, try flying by the seat of your pants. Spend a weekend just making it up as you go along, let someone else plan your next vacation, or sign up for a blind draw tournament where you have no control over who you get to play with. And when it comes to your golf swing, if it *really* isn't up to the level that deserves any faith in it whatsoever, I know about 27,000 PGA Professionals in the U.S. alone who'd love to help.

Now, I understand, especially for you control freaks out there, that finally giving up a little control will be uncomfortable at first, but finding your personal path to doing so can be the key to feeling free. In golf, the ability to control our shots is to a certain degree an illusion. The golf club is moving so fast that even slow swingers cannot actually see where the face is at impact, and the more we try to control where it is, the more it seems to get away from us. We need to believe in our abilities, in the soundness of our mechanics, in the fact that we've done it before, and ultimately trust that only in surrendering a little bit of the control we so desperately wish for will we actually start to get it. That is why, as anyone who has ever taken a lesson from me can attest, I am so fond of saying that in golf, as in life, very often we must *give up control to get control*. And if all that doesn't work, you may just need to change the perceived consequence, loosen that Klingon death grip, and just let it go. Because remember, it's not as if you're actually walking that two-foot wide balance beam from a few floors up!

SEE IT, FEEL IT, TRUST IT

"Clear your mind must be, if you are to discover."
– Master Yoda

In the last chapter, I touched on the idea of trusting your swing, but I realized while doing so that I need to take it a step further and give you an actual process for doing just that. Not long ago there was a golf movie called *Seven Days in Utopia* that chronicled the trials of an aspiring young golf professional and his quest to get his game back. It was an entertaining, if not overly deep movie that followed the young professional on his journey to learn how to get out of his own way, to find his golf swing, and ultimately find himself in the process. I found the movie both enjoyable and interesting, particularly as a golfer. Enjoyable because, well, I'm biased toward any movie that involves the game of golf, and even ones that fall short in their execution get a more charitable review from me simply due to the subject matter. Interesting because one of the central themes was the young golfer being taught an actual process for getting out of his own way that, while slightly over-simplified, in fact mirrors processes used by numerous players on tour both past and present.

See it, feel it, trust it is the movement phrase that the "Golf Yoda," played by Robert Duvall, teaches the central character in the film to help him get his mojo back. *Movement phrase???* I understand that the term may sound a bit foreign to those of you who haven't spent a lot of time around players who play high-level competitive golf, but many players on both the men's and ladies' tours would tell you that this mechanism helps them play golf with their intuitive or subconscious mind. Being able to play with your subconscious mind, as I have mentioned previously, is one of the true keys to playing great golf. And if you were to take a close look at what nearly every top sports psychologist is teaching his or her players, it is at least partially the ability how to do just that. We can't access our true ability while consciously directing ourselves to execute a given athletic motion, and considering the intricacies of a successfully executed golf swing, that is likely no truer in any sport than in golf. So what do we need to learn to do just that?

One of the things I have worked long and hard on with many of my advanced competitive players over the years is to develop a disciplined playing routine. I call this *learning to manage the 21 seconds in-action.* Golf is one of the most sedentary sports, because if you look at how much time you spend engaged in actually playing, it is only about 15 to 20 minutes of the four to five hours that you spend on the course. The in-action routine encompasses the span from when you first stand behind the golf ball with the correct club in your hand and initiate your pre-shot routine, to the space of time you are engaged in swinging to hit the ball, to a brief post-shot period following both successful and unsuccessful shots. I developed the 21 seconds rule while watching video of many successful players engaged in their routines and took what looked to be a pretty compelling average number. But we'll leave out the post-shot period for now and focus on that time leading up to and including the action.

In order to better manage this period of time, the first step you need to take is to develop a disciplined pre-shot routine. The first included element of one should likely be visualization. This is the "see it" portion of your routine. As I've touched on visualization more than once, it should by now be a concept that you are familiar with. And while I think I've covered it enough up to this point for you to appreciate its importance, I maybe haven't exactly painted the process for you. It won't be exactly the same for everyone, but once you stand behind the ball, you want to visualize the precise shot and shot shape that you intend to hit all the way into the hole. This communicates to your body exactly what you intend to do prior to making any rehearsal swings.

Secondly, you have to "feel it." In a literal sense, this is what the rehearsal swing is for, and this space of time is important for reinforcing the actual feel of what you need to do. I am not adamant about whether or not you make one, two, or even three rehearsal swings, as everyone has their own sense of rhythm. What allows you to *feel it* may be different for another, but for most good players, no more than two are necessary on full swings to embed the feel (and possibly one or two additional when you are in areas where you need less than a full swing). What is most important is that during this time you are not only rehearsing the swing you want, but simultaneously recalling the feel of countless successful swings you have made for similar shots in similar situations, and the more recent shots you can bring to mind, the better.

And finally, you have to "trust it." There are some very esoteric internal debates among the real *Golf Yodas* out there (*yawn*) as to what exactly one should be saying to oneself during this time, but this is exactly where the movement phrase comes in handy. The most commonly employed is the movement phrase or swing thought, which is that one final instruction to yourself like "free and easy," "trust it," or "let it go," which is repeated in your mind during the last few seconds before and during your initiation of the swing. Movement phrases should ideally not consist of any precise mechanical instructions like "keep my left arm straight," "tuck my elbow," or "fire the hips," as they will move the act of swinging back into your conscious mind, something that by definition you are trying to avoid when you *trust it*.

An alternative to the swing thought or movement phrase is a mechanism developed by Dr. Carey Mumford, and it is called a *Clear Key*. Clear Keys are to be used during this same time, just prior to and during the initiation of the action (and a great portion of the moments preceding, according to Dr. Mumford), and they have garnered a pretty fair following in competitive golf and other sports. A Clear Key is essentially a random unrelated non-active phrase that helps clear your mind, thus turning over the swing to your subconscious mind. I have heard Clear Keys that are everything from "grass is green" to "if the goose is blue, the horse will eat." Sam Snead used to say "oily" to himself over and over in his head because it brought to mind images of swinging fluidly and essentially helped clear out unwanted thoughts. In Dr. Mumford's world, the exact phrase used is not really important, so long as it is completely devoid of any type of verbiage that would suggest any action on your part and turn the direction of the swing over to the conscious mind.

Whether it ultimately is movement phrase or Clear Key, I find myself perched comfortably upon the fence. I have worked with good players and know professionals who have found value in the use of Clear Keys during this time, yet others struggle a bit and find them distracting, preferring something a little more focused or conceptually related to what they want to accomplish. In the end, your preference will be a personal thing that may take a period of experimentation to decide upon, but I encourage you to play around with both. The important thing is, whether you settle upon a movement phrase or a **Clear Key**, finding something that is predetermined and routine, so that it keeps your mind focused in a way that crowds out the space for unwanted thoughts like conscious direction of your swing or places on the map that you'd rather not see your unfortunate golf ball visiting. Trusting it, by definition, completely accepts and understands that the directions and control of the conscious mind will only tense you up and keep you from swinging freely, easily, and naturally.

So if you've never spent any time on your routine, it might just be time to start planning those 21 seconds in-action by learning to *see it, feel it,* and *trust it.* Because we've all swung the club thousands of times anyway and have a natural swing that by now shouldn't need any conscious direction from us to engage. If we can learn a process that helps us to develop that necessary trust, we may just find that we can finally get out of our own way long enough to allow our natural swings to happen. "The rain in Spain falls mainly on the plain. The rain in Spain falls mainly on the plain. The rain in Spain falls mainly on the plain. The rain in Spain falls mainly on the plain. The rain in Spain falls mainly on the plain. The rain in Spain falls mainly on the plain." You try it!

DANCE WITH WHO YA BRUNG!

"Seldom do people discern eloquence
under a threadbare cloak."

– Juvenal

Down in Texas there's an age-old saying: "You gotta dance with who ya brung!" In the Longhorn State, it is most often attributed to legendary University of Texas football coach Darrel Royal, but there was a book written with a similar title, and (predictably) there's even a country music song by the same name. Growing up in the game of golf, however, I remember it most vividly because it was a standby for the old professional I learned the game from, due to his disdain for practice and even warming up most of the time. While a native Virginian, Southern boy Slammin' Sam Snead was generally credited with popularizing the saying in golf circles, and it was one of the good ol' country boy's favorites throughout his storied career. Unlike most of today's professionals, who seem obsessed with their swings and the never-ending pursuit of perfecting their mechanics, Sam was loathe to tinkering with his swing and hated making last-minute adjustments prior to an event. The three-time Masters champion preferred to go with whatever type of shot his fluid swing was producing that week—or even that day—than to spend any time trying to correct it, and he believed the inability to find a way to score during such times was in and of itself a weakness in one's game.

Many who play the game today could benefit by taking a page from Sam's book and learning to adopt his type of conviction. The art of playing well when you're not swinging well seems to be a lost art at best, and along with that seems to have gone at least some of the desire to even try. We used to admire players like Walter Hagen, Sam Snead, or Seve Ballesteros and their ability to put up a good number even when a good number of their shots were less than pretty. It seems today's players prefer to worship at the altar of precise mechanics, having more reverence for the many technicians that populate today's professional ranks than the artistry and fortitude of many of the players of yesteryear. And the predictable result of this is that the average player today spends his time on the range or during a lesson hitting ball after ball and invariably crying for an explanation of the mechanical breakdown responsible for every less than perfect shot, while barely giving more than a moment's nod to those that *are* successful or the thought of how to deal with the ones that aren't.

I know that, when I claim that many of us seem overly preoccupied with the quest for a perfect swing, I might be starting to sound as if I'm beating the proverbial dead horse. However, if it inspires a little newfound conviction to trust in your abilities, it'll be worth the risk. How and when did we arrive at the point where there is such a preoccupation with perceived swing flaws that most of us seem patently unable to enjoy scraping it around anymore when we're hitting it anything less than perfect? And have we come so far down the road to fixation upon our shortcomings that we can't appreciate and learn to rely upon those talents we actually do possess?

The constant fixation on what is wrong with our swing and our tendency to obsess over missed shots and what we need to do to avoid them is essentially golf's version of *poverty mentality*, a term popularized by the late motivational speaker Zig Ziegler but whose concepts reach much farther back to Buddhist teachings thousands of years old. Poverty mentality is a preoccupation with what one doesn't possess, and in golf it is a real barrier to improvement. It manifests itself in a tendency to be overly fixated on the negative—negative outcomes and circumstances, and in golf it is often the precursor to negative feelings about our swing and our ability to execute acceptable swings. It is a mentality that can be extremely crippling because it typically results in a player's inability to just relax and trust their swing, and players who make tight, anxious swings will never be able to play to their potential, regardless of their level of ability.

The other problem with this poverty mentality is that it robs us of the enjoyment and self-satisfaction so many of golf's challenges can bring. Our friend Albert Einstein once said, "In the middle of difficulty there lies opportunity." Learn to roll with the ups and downs of the game. Begin to look at those difficult situations as not only opportunities to practice becoming your foursome's version of the golfing Houdini, but opportunities to practice the type of mental fortitude that will actually have you looking forward to those difficult situations after a while. It not only helps you become a more complete player, but it really can alleviate some of the pressure of having to hit great shots all the time.

So how do we begin to change our golfer's poverty mentality to one of prosperity? We can start by enlisting the wisdom of The Slammer. The swing we have is the swing we have on any given day, and we would be a lot better served by just trusting it instead of fighting it. We need to have the conviction to save potential swing changes for practice sessions or times spent with our coach, instead of at the last minute on the range before we tee off or, worse yet, during the round after every less than desirable shot. The next thing we can do is to shed that threadbare cloak and start to turn our focus towards the eloquence of all those shots that are not only acceptable, but also possibly even better than expected. Following each less than perfect shot by moaning things like "Stick a fork in me" or "It's just not my day" (and the negative emotions that go with statements like these) releases certain brain chemicals that not only increase our feelings of nervousness and anxiety, but embed the memories of those shots so much so that, before long, visions of bad shots are the only ones you can recall. This is not only a recipe for bad golf, but for players in the habit of doing so, it can eventually become difficult to find anyone willing to play along and listen to it. So listen to Sam and *dance with who ya' brung*, and not only will it help you finally start to relax and enjoy both the ups and the downs of the journey, but it will also help you develop the kind of conviction necessary to truly trust your swing. And once you can do that, you will likely play a bit better, and you might just discover it's a little easier to find a few playing partners willing to enjoy the journey with you.

PART 9

ON VISION, WISDOM,

AND BENEVOLENCE

THE SMELL OF SUCCESS

"Memories, imagination, old sentiments, and associations are more readily reached through the sense of smell than through any other channel."
– Oliver Wendell Holmes

Many years ago, when I was first in the golf business, and long before I had spent much time studying psychology and brain science, I dated a gal who didn't like the game of golf. For at least one very obvious reason, the relationship didn't last, but it is notable because, not long after we had been dating, I was out cutting the lawn one day when she mentioned that she hated the smell of fresh cut grass. Now, most people have smells they don't particularly like, but I hadn't heard of this one before, so something piqued my curiosity. Sensing there was something more behind it, I stopped what I was doing and asked why.

"Oh, I don't know," she said at first, as if she had never really considered the matter before, but then she continued almost immediately. "I guess it's because my parents divorced when I was young, and the last few years before they split up, if my dad wasn't working, he was playing golf. When he finally got home at night, he always smelled of fresh cut grass. You know, he chose playing golf over spending time with his family. God, I hate that smell!" For this young lady, the mere smell of fresh cut grass triggered feelings of anger and abandonment in such a strong way that it instantly brought back some very painful memories.

In the hierarchy of our senses, the sense of smell amazingly is second only to sight in evoking strong feelings and emotions and triggering memories. Scientists have known this for years and refer to it as the *Proust effect*, after French author Marcel Proust. It is the reason why the realtor invariably seems to be pulling a fresh baked batch of chocolate chip cookies out of the oven just moments prior to you arriving for the showing of a home for sale. The smell of cookies, for many, causes us to hearken back to days of our childhood and the warm fuzzy feelings of coming home from school and finding our mothers having done the very same thing just in time for our arrival. A simple smell can instantly transport you to another place and time, affect your feelings about your surroundings, and enhance memory retrieval, and people in advertising and marketing have long been aware of this. Scents and smells travel across your olfactory nerves inside your nose and up to the brain to the part that controls mood, memories, and even your ability to learn. This area of the brain is known as the limbic system, and when stimulated, it can release endorphins and other chemicals that affect heart rate, blood pressure, breathing, memory, stress levels, and hormones—all elements that can affect performance in just about any athletic endeavor.

Now if up until now you have been wondering how all of this might be related to playing better golf, then I'm about to tell you. I've already mentioned that one of the things that I teach and utilize in my teaching to competitive golfers is the power of visualization and how the best golfers and athletes use it to improve their performance. Visualization, however, isn't just visual. The best forms of visualization engage as many of your senses as possible, and combining visual and olfactory senses together is very powerful. How can you do that, when other than that fresh cut grass, the sense of smell is something that you might say the game of golf rarely engages? Well, essential oils and aromatherapy are all the rage these days. There are oils that supposedly help you relax, breathe deeper and better, think more clearly, build your immune system, and a whole host of other things I won't go into. And sensing an opportunity, I guess the world of golf—or at least some people in it—are ready to jump on the bandwagon. A new product that came to market not long ago called Swing Trust Oil, and it combines a number of essential oils that have been formulated to build confidence, release tension, calm the nervous system, reduce anxiety, and provide supportive thoughts and trust, all in one little bottle.

Now, one of the things that I tend to pride myself in is the fact that I am not easily duped. I have an ability, typically, to see through to the heart of the matter on many issues, and when you combine that with a fair amount of knowledge about what it takes to improve in the game of golf, it is no wonder that I am almost instantly skeptical when it comes to products that claim to magically improve your game. To put it another way, when it comes to golf, I know a snake oil salesman when I see one, and when I hear about the majority of these magical cures, I tend to look at them in the same way I do those carnival barkers who tell you how easy it is to knock those lead-filled milk bottles off the pedestal with three baseballs that have the consistency of marshmallows. So are the promises of this product too good to be true? Maybe, but at least one tour player is using and endorsing it, and the more you know about how powerful the sense of smell can be and how it can be used to enhance your visualization, you start to take pause. Maybe you cannot only envision success— maybe you can actually even smell it. And if so, apparently it can be bottled, and for little more than the cost of renting a golf cart these days, *the smell of success* could finally be yours.

HAVE YOU GOT GOLFZHEIMERS?

*"The difference between false memories and true
is the same for gems. It is always the false ones
that look the most real, the most brilliant."*
— Salvador Dali

While it has taken more than a quarter century of teaching golf to arrive at this point, I have recently come to the realization that there is an as-yet-unnamed epidemic condition afflicting a great majority of players. This condition is so prevalent that I think it is high time it had a name, so here in my first book, I want to be the first to navigate those uncharted waters and to give it one in hopes that, once formally recognized, it will begin to be more seriously studied in search for a cure. I will call this condition "Golfzheimers," as it is the complete inability most golfers seem to have to remember the vast majority of the good shots they have ever hit (even those hit only moments before), while having the uncanny ability to instantly recall every chunk, shank, skull, and chili-dip they've hit since sometime back around the time balls were still covered with balata. Now trust me, I am not trying to make light of a very troubling and serious disease. My grandmother is suffering with Alzheimer's, and it is a heartbreaking condition. In truth, if I were just concerned about someone taking offense (and I am truly sorry if you do), I could have just as easily named this the golfer's "Senior Moment," since that term is ubiquitous enough. But it was after a conversation I had with my grandmother a while back that I was suddenly struck with how oddly similar her lack of short-term memory, combined with her ability to vividly remember things that happened 40 or 50 years ago, was in some ways to how most golfers tend to think.

As long as I have been playing and teaching, I have been searching for different ways to learn to accept your bad shots, keep them in perspective, and move on without letting them affect the next shot, hole, or round. When it comes to swinging the golf club, I can generally teach someone how to hit pretty good golf shots in a fairly short period of time, but teaching them to remember them with the same level of clarity as those of the more wayward variety often seems like trying to teach a blind man to see. Despite a general awareness of this phenomenon by most players and its detrimental effect upon your golf game, little has been suggested until now why it exists and what if anything you can do about it. And while research in the field of neuroscience suggests that our brains are hard-wired from the caveman days to catalogue and assign more importance to events that are considered dangerous or threatening, what about the game can have become so dangerous (other than to our egos) that we all seem to be fighting such an uphill battle?

Numerous psychological studies that have been done report that most people can remember five bad experiences more readily than five good ones, and assuming this is true, it speaks a great deal about how we have been conditioned to think since an early age. The concept of *scarcity* has been popularized in the self-help world of late, and it essentially describes a lens through which many of us have been conditioned to look upon our world, our lives, and our games apparently with far too much regularity. It is through the use of this concept that many of our parents kept us at the dinner table as children, far beyond our wishes and long after our dinners were cold. We were guilt-ridden, not because we might be unappreciative of the time and money that went into providing us with that dinner, but because there were millions of starving children in China or some other far-off country that would have been tripping over themselves for even the remnants of that liver and onions our mothers had beset upon us.

As a proud parent, I'm embarrassed to say I've used the scarcity tactic a time or two myself during moments of desperation, but being naturally an optimist, I try to avoid succumbing to its siren song, because I know the road it leads down and prefer to teach my daughters a better lesson. At the same time, however, they are proof positive of these same studies about our ability to recall, which is evidenced by a little game we tend to play at that very same dinner table most nights—a game I like to call *high and low*. A lot of people play the same game; I essentially ask them what their high and low moments were during the day. I ask them to tell me the low first, preferring to close their day's reflection with something positive, but it's uncanny how often recalling something positive makes them really pause and reflect, while if something negative occurred, their recall of it is nearly instant and typically very descriptive.

The good news, however, for both my daughters and the general golfing public, is there is a very effective way to short-circuit this type of thinking, and it comes from the field of hypnosis. From this moment forward, make a point not only to remember every good thing that happens to you, but to stop and savor it. If you are paid a compliment, don't just brush it off. Stop to relish it for a moment and recognize the responsible person with more than just the perfunctory, "Thanks." If you accomplish a goal, regardless of how small, reward yourself in at least some small way, all the while reminding yourself how good it feels to follow through on your intentions. And if you actually hit a golf shot well, reflect a moment, make a point to enjoy it and remember the moment vividly, and actually thank your partners when they say "Nice shot," rather than blowing it off with some sort of "Even a blind squirrel finds an acorn once in a while" type of comment. Hitting the golf ball well is a near miraculous achievement when you consider the complexity of the swing and the incredible timing and hand-eye coordination it requires. Enjoy it (or anything else for that matter) when it actually comes off right. Do this several times a day for a month or more and there will be subtle changes in your brain chemistry, how you feel, and your outlook on life. You will notice, and so will those closest to you. Make it a long-term habit and it's very likely you'll avoid ever having your playing partners ask that dreaded question, *"Have you got Golfzheimers?"*

SEND A SELF-ADDRESSED LETTER

"By three methods we may learn wisdom: First, by reflection, which is noblest; Second, by imitation, which is easiest; and third by experience, which is bitterest."

– Confucius

Every once in a while, you read something that really stops you for a moment. When a writer is able to do that, to write something powerful, insightful, or witty enough that it causes you to laugh, cry, reflect, or think in way that you wouldn't normally, it makes you want to share it. A few years ago, I attended a teaching workshop that was given by a man named Fred Shoemaker, who has written what I believe are some of the more ground-breaking golf books (*Extraordinary Golf* and

Extraordinary Putting). Now, I enjoy writing and hope that I at least, now an then, come up with a few noteworthy pearls of wisdom to ponder, but there is a passage in Fred's first book that I believe was so well written that I want to share it with you in its full unedited form. In it, Fred claims that if most golfers were able to somehow miraculously take a trip into the future and write a letter to their younger self as a golfer, he imagines that it would likely sound a little something like this...

Dear Younger Me,

I can't play golf anymore. I tried to swing the club the other day, but my body wouldn't cooperate. The best I can do now is sometimes take walks on the course, but my eyes aren't as good as they used to be so I don't see much. I have a lot of time to sit and think now, and I often think about the game.

It was my favorite game. I played most of my adult life. Thousands of rounds, thousands of hours practicing. As I look back, I guess I had a pretty good time at it. But now that I can't do it anymore, I wish I had done it differently.

It's funny, but with all the time I spent playing golf, I never thought I was a real golfer. I never felt good enough to really belong out there. It doesn't make much sense, since I scored better than average and a lot of people envied my game, but I always felt that if I was just a little better or a little more consistent, then I'd feel really good. I'd be satisfied with my game. But I never was. It was always "One of these days I'll get it" or "One day I'll get there" and now here I am. I can't play anymore, and I never got there.

I met a whole lot of different people out on the course. That was one of the best things about the game. But aside from my regular partners and a few others, I don't feel like I got to know many of those people very well. I know they didn't really get to know me. At times they probably didn't want to. I was pretty occupied with my own game most of the time and didn't have much time for anyone else, especially if I wasn't playing well.

So why am I writing you this letter anyway, just to complain? Not really. Like I said, my golfing experience wasn't that bad. But it could have been so much better, and I see that so clearly now. I want to tell you, so you can learn from it. I don't want you getting to my age and feeling the same regrets I'm feeling now.

I wish, I wish. Sad words, I suppose, but necessary. I wish I could have played the game with more joy, more freedom. I was always so concerned with "doing it right" that I never seemed to be able to enjoy just doing it at all. I was so hard on myself, never satisfied, always expecting more. Who was I trying to please? Certainly not myself, because I never did. If there were people whose opinions were important enough to justify all that self-criticism, I never met them.

I wish I could have been a better playing partner. I wasn't a bad person to be with, really, but I wish I had been friendlier and gotten to know people better. I wish I could have laughed and joked more and given people more encouragement. I probably would have gotten more from them, and I would have loved that. There were a few bad apples over the years, but most of the people I played with were friendly, polite, and sincere. They really just wanted to make friends and have a good time. I wish I could have made more friends and had a better time.

I'm inside a lot now and I miss the beauty of the outdoors. For years when I was golfing I walked through some of the most beautiful places on earth, and yet I don't feel I really saw them. Beautiful landscapes, trees, flowers, animals, the sky, and the ocean – how could I have missed so much? What was I thinking of that was so important – my grip, my backswing, my stance? Sure, I needed to think about those sometimes, but so often as to be oblivious to so much beauty? And all the green – the wonderful, deep, lush color of green! My eyes are starting to fail. I wish I had used them better so I would have more vivid memories now.

So what is it that I'm trying to say? I played the type of game that I thought I should play, to please the type of people that I thought I should please. But it didn't work. My game was mine to play, but I gave it away. It's a wonderful game. Please, don't lose yours. Play a game that you want to play. Play a game that gives you joy and satisfaction and makes you a better person to your family and friends. Play with enthusiasm, play with freedom. Appreciate the beauty of nature and the people around you. Realize how lucky you are to be able to do it. All too soon your time will be up, and you won't be able to play anymore. Play a game that enriches your life.

That's all I have to say. I don't really know how this letter will get to you, but I hope that it reaches you in time. Take care,

Love, The Older Me

When I first read this, it really caused me to think. And upon reflection, I suppose that writing this book has been my own little way of sending this letter to you. Golf is a game, but it is really so much more than that. Golf is a way of life and one that I am incredibly grateful for. So if in some small way, any of these things I have written up until now or hereafter have made you laugh, cry, reflect, or think a little bit deeper about what the game means to you and how you can enjoy it more, then I will have succeeded. I hope that is the case and that at some point you have or will similarly *send a self-addressed letter.*

TAKE THE ROAD LESS TRAVELLED

"Out of the mouths of babes and sucklings thou hast perfected praise."
– Matthew 21:16

You don't have to have kids or even have spent a tremendous amount of time with them to know that, as Art Linkletter once said, "Kids say the darndest things." Well, I was hit square in the face with this at breakfast one morning when my youngest daughter, who was three at the time and had taken to getting up early with me as I got ready for work, would plead with me not to go and ask me essentially why I had to.

"Well, a lot of people want to learn how to play golf, honey, and Daddy has to go teach them how," I explained, trying to put it into as simple terms as possible so that she would understand.

She looked at me with a curiously puzzled look that belied her years and replied, "Why, Daddy? They just swing their arms..." Even though it was 6:00 A.M. and the rest of the family was fast asleep, I couldn't help but laugh out loud when she said it, but then the realization hit me of how potentially profound her statement really was. Golf is a simple game, really. You put a round ball into a round hole in the least number of strokes possible. Is it possible that some of us at some point have made it out to be more difficult than it really is? Is it possible that we've so overanalyzed the process that we've become disconnected from its natural simplicity, a process so basic that, from a child's unencumbered perception, it is just swinging your arms? And have we become so hypnotized by the grace and beauty of a well-executed golf swing that we've completely bought into the idea that mastery of its mechanics is the holy grail of playing great golf? Well, at least in some respects, I believe that today this can largely be argued to be the case, but my ultimate arrival at that conclusion required a journey down "the road less travelled."

I grew up in the game as mostly a self-taught feel player. No one in my family other than my grandfather played regularly, and I only had a handful of basic lessons but managed to become a reasonably accomplished high school player through a highly sophisticated routine of just playing golf and hitting some balls now and then before going out. The game came fairly easy to me early on and seemed pretty simple, and I was typically able to fix anything that was not working in about five minutes on the practice tee before my round or at least during the first couple of holes. I enjoyed it immensely, and while I played in tournaments with some of degree of success and definitely wanted to do more, I don't think I ever really felt the need to overanalyze how or what I was doing at the time.

This all changed, however, shortly after I took a position at the local country club and turned professional at the age of 20. The bloom was off the rose. The more I learned about the golf swing and how difficult this game really is, the more newfound difficulties I seemed to have with my own game and I was only mildly comforted with the fact that nearly everyone in my profession seemed to struggle with similar issues at one time or another.

My early career was spent working for and learning from a professional whose teaching philosophy was very technical (being from the Mac O'Grady/Homer Kelley Golf Machine School of thought). This was in contrast to my simpler approach, and in retrospect, I suppose it's no small wonder that I seemed to regularly pick up students who would come away from his lessons cross-eyed with the overwhelming complexity of trying to make a golf club hit Mac's umpteen positions with precision during the swing. At the time, however, I still failed to fully recognize or question the underlying issue at hand. How could the accumulation of knowledge, particularly intricate knowledge about the nature of what it takes to properly swing a golf club, actually hurt my game and that of my colleagues and students? I had heard the term *paralysis from analysis,* but at the time that seemed a half-humorous and gross oversimplification, and it would be many years before I began to put the pieces of the puzzle together.

The first piece hit me as a result of an experience had by that very same overly analytical, overly mechanical head professional at one of our section PGA tournaments. One of the more accomplished players among our club professional ranks, one who had qualified for and played in numerous U.S. Opens and PGA Championships, was hitting shots from the practice bunker before the round and landing them as soft as the proverbial butterfly with sore feet all around the pin. Numerous other pros stood close by as in a trance, watching his prowess as if trying to absorb some of his ability. It was my boss, however, who approached him upon his exit from the bunker, having built up enough courage to ask a question.

"Excuse me, Bob," he said. "If you don't mind me asking, what are you thinking about when you're hitting that shot?" Now, in my boss's mind, I'm quite sure the gears of mechanics and positions were turning. He was looking for a very technical answer that would explain the complexity of the process in a way he could absorb and assimilate into his own game and teachings.

The answer he got, however, after a sort of puzzled look that only now seems eerily similar to my three-year-old's at the breakfast table was, "Gee, Steve, I don't know."

Could it really be that simple? Could it be in fact that the most skilled among us could execute such a complex athletic motion without even being consciously aware of how? Upon hearing this, it suddenly occurred to me that this was how I used to play—in a sort of state of blissful ignorance that was scarcely aware of the process of how I played. I just did. Could I get back there? Could I teach other people to do the same? Thus began a long and winding journey down many different paths, some of which I had up to that point been unaware even existed.

My next steps saw me embark upon a quest to seek out teachers whose swing philosophy was somewhat simpler and who espoused a more natural approach. I loved the golf swings of Ben Hogan and Freddy Couples and was impressed by the complexity of Homer Kelley's Golfing Machine, but somehow I knew that overvaluing the mechanics of any given motion was, in and of itself, a dead-end road. Thirty-plus years of study had founded a cottage industry around the idea of discovering the elusive "secret" to Ben Hogan's prodigious ball-striking, yet no one seemed any closer to putting the pieces of the puzzle together.

So I started to look elsewhere and began attending seminars given by the legendary Bill Strausbaugh and Michael Hebron, reading the latter's book *See and Feel the Inside Move the Outside* until the pages were dog-eared and torn. I studied Dean Reinmuth's *Tension-Free Golf* and attended still more schools and seminars. The more I learned about the golf swing, the more it confirmed for me that it really wasn't all about the golf swing. And I began to sense that I wasn't alone. While most golf schools and golf instructors at the time were stuck on a model or a formulaic method for teaching what they thought was the right swing, a slow-moving realization began to steadily take shape—a realization that in our quest to solve the golf swing, to unlock the mysteries of this extremely complex physical motion, the industry had at some point taken such a definitive fork in the road that it was unable to see the forest for the trees.

Sure, there was something to be learned from unraveling the mystery that surrounded men like Ben Hogan and a golf swing that approached automaticity. And understandably, a mystique inevitably surrounds a reclusive character like Moe Norman, the autistic Canadian whose legendary ability to strike a golf ball repetitively seems only added to by his disdain for putting and playing tournament golf. But to found entire schools of golf around the replication of their unique swings seemed almost foolish to me. Wasn't each person an individual, with unique physical capabilities, a unique body type, and a unique sense of personal rhythm that was all their own? If so, it seemed only natural there could be no one exact right way to swing the golf club. Hadn't hundreds, maybe thousands of different individuals over the years succeeded at the highest levels, while all in possession of golf swings as different and unique to them as their fingerprints? And if the answers to both of these questions was yes, then the next and most obvious question was—if the most successful golfers in history didn't have golf swings in common, what *did* they share?

Given my simultaneous realizations about the many differences among successful golf swings, my next steps took an only slightly unexpected turn in 1994 when I attended a workshop given by Dr. Glen Albaugh. Dr. Albaugh was a former University of the Pacific coach and sports psychologist who had begun working primarily with golfers hoping to play professionally and whose most high-profile client, Scott McCarron (who was in attendance), had just successfully qualified for the PGA Tour. Even back then, it was pretty much accepted that the difference between the guys that made it out on tour each year and the thousands of others who tried was mental toughness. At that level, they all possessed good golf swings in one form or another, so there obviously had to be other reasons that determined the makeup of the cream that rose to the top. And as much as I didn't want to admit it, I had slowly begun to realize that my own playing career had likely stalled more because of shortcomings in my own mental game than any inherent swing flaws.

Despite my ever-increasing acceptance of these facts, for some reason I hadn't begun any search for answers in earnest. My only explanation for that, I suppose, was that I had yet to be exposed to anyone who had any concrete thoughts, ideas, or methods for doing anything about it. The state of the industry was for the most part centered on a prevailing notion that you either had it or you didn't, so very few were exploring the idea of how you could get it. The field of psychology had only recently transcended its stereotypical image of the patient lying on a couch while being interrogated by some Freudian character with a notepad and pencil to make some inroads into athletics and golf in particular. And from my ignorant standpoint, the majority opinion at the time seemed to be that sports psychologists might help the weak, the feeble, and possibly those with some sort of a mental block like the yips, but they didn't really offer things that those at the highest level of performance didn't already innately possess. In one short day, however, I felt I had been given the proverbial "keys to the kingdom," and for me, all that changed.

I wound up that day in the same small group of four with Scott McCarron. Here was someone I was at least a little familiar with, having played with him once and whose game I knew a little about because while he was a few years older than me. I had friends who had grown up playing competitively against him before he went to the University of Southern California. Now he was on tour, and the fact that he was on tour he was attributing not to his God-given gifts of ability and mental toughness, but largely to a handful of mental game techniques that he had learned from Dr. Albaugh. And here in Dr. Albaugh was someone who was claiming to be able to teach these techniques to anyone. I'm at least a little bit Danish and at that point figured I'd been around long enough to know when *something was rotten in the state of Denmark,* but this was a new concept to me. I began to think that maybe what I thought I knew about the mental game barely scratched the surface.

The following spring, Dr. Bob Rotella released his first book, *Golf is Not a Game of Perfect*, and I began to sense a subtle shift in not only my own attitude about the subject, but among those in my profession, the industry, and the general golfing public. But there was still a long way to go. I had spotted the tip of the iceberg but knew it was going to take some exploring beneath the waterline to discover what I was really dealing with. I hadn't exactly given up on the idea that one's golf swing might be the thing that ultimately separates them from what they want to achieve in the game, and I am still an avid student of swing theory today. It's just that I suddenly realized that there were so many other unexplored possibilities related to the mental side of the game and our personal development that at least stood on equal footing when it came to that ultimate success, and I wanted to investigate those possibilities.

I want to stop here and say I never intended to recount every step along that winding road in this little tale because not only do I think it more important to understand how I got there, but that would literally be another book in and of itself. Just know that while in the years since this revelation I have made uncountable discoveries, filled with innumerable "a-ha moments" (the results of which do fill many of the chapters of *this* book), this isn't a journey that is nearly finished. It has been a process that continues to evolve and unfold in front of me and a journey that I expect will never really be over. To this point there hasn't been any one source, book, or individual who has inspired me and shaped my philosophy more than any other, but rather a vast collection of resources, research, and experiences that is ever growing. With the evolution of the Internet, there is now an incredible amount of information, articles, research, sites, columns, and video at your fingertips. This is not to say that it is all good information, but the sheer volume and ease of availability makes researching the game and finding different points of view easier than ever before. My library of golf, sports psychology, psychology, personal development, and behavioral and brain science books and articles seems to grow almost daily, and subsequently the insight into performance I have gained has grown exponentially. These insights, along with the continual observation and experiences with my own students, have succeeded in shaping my views on instruction, coaching, and achievement in ways that I hadn't before imagined.

And so in the end you might ask what wisdom I have ultimately acquired as a result of this journey. Well, much hopefully, but I will say that at least to this point I have arrived at what I believe is one single overriding conclusion. As long as people have played golf, they have been involved in a search for the holy grail of better golf, and just as in history's well-chronicled search for the actual holy grail, this search has been riddled with deceptions, real clues, false hopes, occasional breakthroughs, and dead ends. And as one who has played a small a part in the search, at least one thing has become clear:

there is no holy grail. But with an indomitable spirit, still we press on in hopes of finding it, so in the interest of hope, I offer you all this. While there is no one holy grail, there does exist a veritable treasure trove of potentially sacred and valuable things that are virtually hiding in plain sight. And I hope that I have given you at least a few places to start looking, because I know from experience that the understanding and application of many of these things offer us all a better chance of improving our golf, our life, and our enjoyment of the journey. So while each of us may start in a different place and each of our unique journeys will likely take a slightly different path, at least we can feel comforted in the fact today that if we'd like to "take the road less travelled," there's a far better roadmap than there ever used to be if you're willing to look at it.

GIVE THE GIFT OF GOLF

"Give a man a fish you feed him for a day; teach a man to fish and you feed him for a lifetime."
– Maimonides

Every year when leaves begin to fall and a chill is in the air, we are reminded (earlier and earlier by the retail industry, it seems) that the season of giving is nearly at hand. And for us parents of young children, the impending arrival of Santa and all the bounty our young ones expect to receive present us with a myriad of potential teaching moments that we can't afford to pass up. And because of that fact, it typically isn't long before you will hear at least one of us trotting out that old standby, "It's better to give than to receive." Well, I truly believe that to be true, as I personally find little more satisfying than when you find that perfect gift for someone and get to see their expression when they first realize they've been given something they truly appreciate.

Whether you're a parent in search of a teachable moment or not, however, the arrival of the holidays can make us all keenly aware of just how many people are in need, and you needn't look too hard to find plenty of worthwhile charities and organizations that could use your help. From the Salvation Army bell-ringers that stand vigil in front of our preferred retail outlets to the canned food drives at our local churches to the numerous Toys For Tots-type initiatives and telethons on TV, in no other time of year are these organizations and their causes so front and center, potentially presenting us with a dilemma. If we are so inclined, which of these organizations and causes most deserves our support? Well, in my opinion, one of the most rewarding things is when you find the perfect combination of a charity whose cause you believe in and a gift that keeps on giving. As a golfer and someone who actively volunteers in the community, I believe this combination couldn't be more perfectly aligned than it is in The First Tee.

For those of you unfamiliar with it, in 1997, the LGPA, Masters Tournament, PGA of America, PGA Tour, and USGA formed a partnership, with the help of Shell Oil, to start an initiative called The First Tee. It originally began as a way to bring the game of golf to kids that otherwise would not be exposed to it and its positive values. What began as a concept whose goal was to make golf more accessible to young people turned into an organization whose mission has grown into helping young people develop core values and skills that are inherent not only to the game of golf, but to the game of life and what it takes to be successful in both. They do this through instilling what they call the **Nine Core Values** (honesty, integrity, sportsmanship, respect, perseverance, confidence, courtesy, responsibility, and judgment), **Nine Healthy Habits** (energy, play, safety, vision, mind, family, school, community, and friends), and a comprehensive code of conduct that includes respect for self, others, and surroundings. And they do all of this while mixing in a little golf instruction and providing a safe and fun environment in which to do it. To date this organization has touched over 7 million young people, with a goal of 10 million by 2017.

Close to my home, The First Tee of Central Valley—our own local chapter—operates the Muni Golf Course in Modesto, but they (as do most other First Tee chapters around the country) have satellite groups throughout Stanislaus and Merced Counties, so if you are interested in getting involved in your community or at least finding out more about it, you likely won't have to go too far. I was fortunate enough to attend their tenth anniversary celebration a couple of years ago, which highlighted the great work they are doing to grow the game and change the lives of kids, many of whom would likely never be otherwise exposed to the game. These are kids who often aren't exposed to the sort of environment and role models from whom they can learn the important life skills that The First Tee teaches and instills. In light of this, it was only slightly surprising to me that night when a young man named Max (who couldn't have been more than six or seven) came up to me on his own and not only introduced himself, but shook my hand and thanked me for supporting The First Tee. In 25 years of giving interviews to prospective employees, I'm not sure I have had one make a stronger first impression (or give a firmer handshake). It is easy to see not just how The First Tee is growing the game and helping to ensure it has an even brighter future, but how they are investing in our communities by helping to develop our youth into the citizens we will so desperately need in the future.

So by now I know at least some of you may be thinking, *Yeah, yeah, sounds great and all, but how's this supposed to help my game?* Well, sometimes we need to stop and realize, especially during the season of giving, that by helping *the* game, we are helping *our* game. So when you are looking around next holiday season at the innumerable valuable charities and organizations that need your support, think first of The First Tee and *give the gift of golf* to someone who might not get it otherwise. Not only because it will help to ensure the game we all love has a vibrant future, but also because it will be a gift that will surely give you something back. You can do this through their website at thefirsttee.org or by contacting your local chapter. Have more time than money? Not to worry—you can always become a volunteer, as they are looking for helping hands and they are happy to train. I am always fond of saying that *golf is life*, but in this situation it can really make a life, which makes this a truly unique opportunity—a chance to introduce the game we all love to some who may need it most and who can benefit from it for a lifetime.

SHARE THE GAME

*"What we do for ourselves dies with us. What we do
for others and the world remains and is immortal."*
– Albert Pine

There is a very old joke out there that seems to annually
make the rounds in nearly every 19th hole whose punch-line is,
"Golf is not a matter of life and death—it's much more important
than that." Well, every so often something happens that makes
you reflect on the things that really are important in life and
maybe—just maybe—why it's so important we play this silly
game in the first place.

If you asked people to make a list of the most important
things in life, it would likely be headed by things like God,
family, friends, career, health, and happiness. I may have missed

a few others that come to your mind, but the point is that when faced with compiling a list of the big picture things in life, most people would likely be quick to write off things like sports, games, and pastimes as trivial or, at the very least, would be tempted to place them much farther down the list. Subsequently, one might conclude that golf (or any other sport for that matter) is ultimately unimportant. I, for one, would argue to the contrary.

Sports, games, and pastimes are inexorably connected to just about all of our big picture items in life. And while a fulfilling career can be rewarding and contributes to our sense of well-being, it is for the time spent with the people we care about most and the opportunity to recreate with them that the great majority of us work as long and as hard as we do in the first place. The biggest source of our happiness is often tied to how we spend our leisure time, and if you're reading this, that leisure time and that recreation likely go hand in hand in this game of golf. It is time that my father and grandfather shared with me at a very young age and time that in turn I am fortunate enough now to share with my two young daughters.

So whether you call it a sport, a game, or a simply a pastime, golf is uniquely important in what it offers to those who engage in it compared to anything else you might so categorize. There are few other things in life that we do for recreation that pay as many dividends as the game of golf. Certainly golf is uniquely positioned as the only athletic endeavor that provides an opportunity for exercise, entertainment, and fair competition between people of every age, gender, and ability level, but that is just barely scratching the surface.

Golf teaches important life lessons, often to those who might not otherwise learn them, in ways unlike any other game—things such as patience, composure, discipline, honor, integrity, and humility. Golf gives back, helping to make higher education possible for many who couldn't afford it, is a source of employment for millions, and provides financial viability to charities of every sort at a level greater than all other sports combined. It brings people together from every race, generation, and ethnicity, lowers barriers while facilitating the building of trust in the business world, and helps develop camaraderie and teamwork among coworkers, unlike any other activity could. It forms new friendships and rekindles old ones, bonds parent with child and sibling alike, and does this all in a setting that brings us closer to the beauty of the world in which we live. But possibly most important of all, golf—as if it knows what's good for us more than we do ourselves—forces us in a world of ever-faster pace to invest the time and slow down just long enough to experience and appreciate all of these things. Yes, golf is important, but regrettably it sometimes takes something unfortunate (even for us so used to singing its praises) to stop and reflect on just how important it really is.

This is what happened to me a few years ago when my father was forced to undergo an emergency surgery to remove a life-threatening cancerous tumor. And while my father was an avid golfer, when I was initially made aware of what needed to happen, golf was truly the furthest thing from my mind. The day of that surgery, however, its true significance came into sharp focus, as I needed look no further than the waiting room to see how important the game of golf really had been for him. Every single one of the seven friends that came to wait with us during the entire nine hours of the procedure and support him and my mother were not just friends, but friends that they golfed with and whom they had met through playing the game. Not one of my father's or mother's long-time coworkers were there, nor their neighbors, friends from church, or even those from the community they had lived in, worked in, played in, and volunteered in for over 30 years were present. But when the chips were down, the friends they had made through the game were there for them, not just that day, but throughout the long ordeal that was to come.

As I mentioned, my father was an avid golfer, and sitting in that waiting room, it didn't take long for me to come to the realization that if he was to make it through that surgery, getting back on the golf course to spend time with my mom, his boys, and especially all those friends who showed up would be the big thing that would drive him to recover from the ordeal. He needed the game (that and the New York Mets), and I have seen many like him in my more than 25 years in the golf business. If for no other reason than the fact that it gave him hope and a light at the end of the tunnel to reach for, I am glad that someone shared the game with him many years ago. And while he ultimately lost his battle, he never lost his love for the game, and those friends were always there supporting him as he attempted to play up until the moment his body just wouldn't let him do so anymore.

Fast-forward to today and we find ourselves at a time when the game of golf itself could use a few new players. Whether it be financial issues, generational issues, or just the evolution of life in an increasingly fast-paced world, we find that fewer and fewer of us over the past few years seem willing to invest the time it takes to play. And for a game that gives so much back to those who play, I think it is an investment that most of us can ill-afford not to make. In light of this, I would ask you to take a moment and think about who you might be able to share the game with. Whether it be a neighbor, a coworker, a child, a grandchild, a brother, sister, father, or mother, I am pretty confident you won't regret it and both of your lives will be so much better for it. And who knows? Some day your life might just depend on it. Thank you, Dad, for sharing this game with me and for giving me the incredible opportunity to do so with others. And thanks in advance to all of you, for doing what I know you will do to *share the game* with others, helping to ensure it remains vibrant and viable for all of us in the many years to come.

PART 10

ON LOVE, GRATITUDE,

AND APPRECIATION

LOVE YOUR GAME

"Sometimes the heart sees what is invisible to the eye."
– H. Jackson Brown Jr.

Millions of people worldwide profess to love the game of golf, yet it would not be too far a stretch to say that for many it is a love/hate relationship. The spiritual leader and motivational speaker Deepak Chopra, in his book *Golf for Enlightenment*, recounts how this paradox initially hooked him on the game. While sitting next to a man on a cross-country flight who was constantly on his phone checking tee times, checking in with golf partners, and thumbing through golf magazines, Chopra posed a casual question to the man in a half-hearted attempt at conversation.

"You must really love the game," Chopra said.

"I think I almost hate it," he replied. "I obsess about golf and I walk off the course mad as hell. My scores don't go down.

Nobody can talk to me without getting an earful of my whining. It's the worst thing I'll never let go of."

In that last sentence, the unnamed man very accurately captured a sentiment that is all too familiar for many golfers, at least from time to time. We are in a deeply committed relationship with a game that often seems to cause us as much frustration as it gives us pleasure. It hooks us early and sets its hooks so deep that for many that relationship can border on obsession. It reminds me of one oft-told joke in which a wife, fed up with how much time her husband spends playing and practicing the game, confronts him with an ultimatum.

"It's either me or the game!" she says in a moment of frustration.

"I'm sure gonna miss her," he says when recounting the situation to his friends later in the clubhouse bar. And while it might sound a bit farcical on the surface, I can tell you from experience that I know of more than one relationship that ended precisely for that reason.

While an accurate depiction of how many of us occasionally feel about the game, that love/hate relationship can also be part of what keeps us from getting better, and getting better is exactly what most of us spend a lifetime trying to do. Whatever we endeavor to do in life, most of us believe in the assumption that continual striving with the intention towards betterment should eventually pay dividends. When that rate of improvement stalls, however, for whatever reason, we can become frustrated and occasionally disillusioned. And it is at times like these that I believe it is becoming increasingly evident that if we want to really improve our games (or whatever else we are striving for), we need to focus on the first half of that love/hate relationship: love.

The heart is tremendously powerful. It is the center of the system that runs your body. At the Institute of HeartMath in the San Francisco Bay Area, scientists have been doing research into the benefits of feeling love, gratitude, and appreciation in your heart, and the results are astounding. Doing these things boosts your immune system, increases important brain chemical production, reduces the production of stress hormones, increases vitality, lowers your blood pressure, reduces anxiety, alleviates burnout, and can even improve blood glucose regulation. Feeling love even improves the rhythm of your heart. These same scientists have shown that the magnetic field of the heart is 5,000 times more powerful than the magnetic field of the brain and reaches out several feet from your body.

At the same time, researchers in Russia, Japan, Europe, and the U.S. have been doing experiments on the effects of love on water. Your body is made up of 70 percent water, and your brain and the inside of your head is made up of over 80 percent water. This would obviously point to the necessity to stay hydrated, but these same scientists have shown that when water is exposed to words and feelings of love, gratitude, and positivity, the energy level of the water increases, and the structure of it changes to become more harmonious. Expose that same water to negative feelings, and it does the opposite, with its energy level dropping substantially and its structure becoming chaotic. If your emotions can change the structure of water, then theoretically they have the ability to change your body down to the cellular level, as each cell of your body is not only filled with water, but requires it to survive.

These are just some of the highlights of the research being done, but if all these facts and figures haven't at least opened your eyes a bit as to the potential benefits of focusing on feelings of love and their promise of at least making you feel better, than let me offer this line of reasoning. At least one PGA Tour mental game coach is now incorporating HeartMath's cutting-edge technology as a core tenet of his emotional management program for players. Teaching players how to manage stress and their emotions by learning to change their heart rhythm patterns helps improve decision-making, fosters positivity, increases trust, and keeps players in the moment. And while members of my club are fortunate enough to be within an hour's drive of a practitioner, each of us can learn to practice many of the tenets of their program without having to leave the comforts of home.

You can get started by learning to be the master of your emotions, rather than being slave to them. I know—easier said than done for some of us, but as I've said before, the reality is that positivity and happiness are choices that you make in each moment, and the easiest path to making those choices is to ensure that everything you do comes from a place of love. Our hearts truly can allow us to see what our eyes have heretofore been blinded to, and from a perspective of love, the game's frustrations don't look quite as frustrating. All those things that were previously trying can become valuable opportunities to increase our appreciation when things actually go right. Bad rounds and poor scores aren't disappointments but rather cherished learning experiences that will teach you what you need to know to succeed the next time around. And annoying partners aren't really annoying when we chose to love them for the lessons in patience they can teach us and for highlighting how truly valuable good playing partners can be. I could go on and on, but I think you get my point. The game so obviously already gives us innumerable reasons to love it, and with just a small change in perspective, any frustrations we have with it that might cause us to momentarily think *I hate this *$@#&% game!* could actually serve to increase our love and appreciation for it that much more. And when you begin to truly love *everything* about your relationship with the game—the good and the bad, the trying and rewarding, the enlightening and the disheartening—not only will the game start to become a little bit easier, but you will truly start to *love your game*. Come to think of it, that approach might help a lot of the other relationships we have in our lives, as well.

KICK THE BUCKET (LIST)

"Love the life you live, live the life you love."
– Bob Marley

In 2007 Jack Nicholson and Morgan Freeman starred in the now-iconic movie, *The Bucket List*, and ever since, the term *bucket list* has become the generally accepted metaphor for things you should do before you die. During that same time, it has also evolved into a generic adjective used to describe the types of places, events, experiences, and accomplishments that you must visit, be a part of, or undertake in order to lead a truly full life. Google *bucket list* and you will get over 74 million results and a cornucopia of ideas for things that would qualify as worthy of the description. Bucket list travel destinations include the Pyramids of Egypt, Machu Picchu in Peru, the Great Wall of

China, or India's Taj Mahal. The events usually include Mardi Gras or Carnivale, Oktoberfest in Germany, and New Year's Eve in Times Square. The experiences might be diving the Great Barrier Reef, going skydiving or bungee-jumping, standing atop the Eiffel Tower, or being a part of the annual Running of the Bulls in Pamplona, Spain. And finally, any self-respecting list would be incomplete without at least a few major accomplishments like scaling Mount Everest, earning an advanced degree, learning to play the guitar, or acting in a Broadway play.

As golfers, however, we typically have our own brand of once-in-a-lifetime experiences, and while they may look a bit different than the average person's, they include things that are just as spectacular, important, personal, or even spiritual to us as those others are to everyone else. Love historic courses? Playing St. Andrews, Carnoustie, Pebble Beach, or Cypress Point would be on any golfer's list. For others, joining a country club, taking a lesson from a top-100 instructor, or playing a round with a golfing icon like Jack Nicklaus, Phil Mickelson, or Tiger Woods might rank higher. More of a spectator? Going with friends or family to watch the Masters, the Ryder Cup, or any other major championship is certainly bucket list-worthy, while making a hole-in-one, playing to a single-digit handicap, winning the club championship, or some other similar event are definitely things that would make just about any golfer's career a bit more fulfilling once it's all said and done.

I think *The Bucket List* was a really good movie, but the reason I believe it succeeded in touching so many people and became so iconic is that it caused us to be introspective, to ask ourselves questions, and to question some of society's commonly held conventions about what is truly important in life. For me, it really begs the question of why it so often takes a terminal illness or the death of a loved one (or a Hollywood movie) for us to stop for a moment and think about these things or try to figure out what we love most about life and what is most important to us. There are lots of reasons, but one of the biggest is that, regardless of our age, a great many of us suffer from the stubbornly persistent delusion that each and every night we to go to sleep, we will rise as predictably as the sun the next morning. As a result, we kick our proverbial can (or bucket list) down the road, believing in a mystical someday, a day when we will have more free time, more money, or both. The problem is, before we know it, that someday is here, and we've never even taken the time to figure out which things are truly most important to us— or even if we have, we've never made a plan for making them happen.

In truth, thinking about these things isn't all that bad, and it can actually be fun and invigorating to ponder our bucket lists (with the possible exception of the whole death part). It's typically a rumination about the types of goals, dreams, and other things that get us out of bed every morning and motivate us to work hard, take care of ourselves, and plan for the future. We've all likely had at least a few of these ideas tucked away somewhere in the back of our minds, even if we haven't gone through the exercise of putting together a list. It's those three or four things that, if asked about, you can rattle off the top of your head, but you've just never gone so far as to write them down or put the wheels in motion that will make them happen.

So with that in mind, here is my suggestion, and while it may seem obvious at this point, I think it's worthwhile to go through the exercise. First, you must resolve to stop kicking your bucket list down the road and get started. Start with the list, and make it an exercise that you do with those who are closest to you, those whom you would most likely be sharing those experiences with. You'll likely begin with your spouse or your family, but it can also be a fun thing to do with a group of buddies while sharing an adult beverage around the 19th hole. Throw everything out there, even those things that might at first sound ridiculous, and once you've each got at least 20 or 30 things on the list, start sorting them into experiences you can share and ones that are more individual or personal. The next thing you do is to find out which things (most likely on your shared list) that you have in common, and put together a shared list for everyone involved. Once you've got that list compiled, rank them in order from hardest to easiest, with the most difficult or challenging things to do right at the top. This might sound a bit radical, but these are the things you focus on first and plan to make happen sooner rather than later.

Believe me, I understand how tempting it will be at first to reach for the low-hanging fruit and to defer the most difficult, but while starting with the most challenging things first might sound a little crazy, there are three really good reasons why you should do so. First of all, larger goals are more motivating and more likely to get you to take action. Especially on the group side, where you have the extra momentum of a shared goal and the likely resulting peer pressure to help ensure that you follow through. You and your golfing buddies might not manage to give up a weekend all together to go see the local PGA Tour event, but you will set aside vacation time, start saving money, and doing extra special honey-dos all year long if it means a hall pass to take a boys' trip to next year's Masters.

Secondly, in today's fast-paced world, it's unfortunately common for many spouses who've been together, even for decades, to have never really spent extended quality time together. I know one couple who spent their 20s, 30s, 40s, and 50s working hard and raising a family, all the while looking forward to a year of traveling the U.S. by motorhome upon retirement. Well, they finally got there and headed out on the road, making it all of six weeks before returning and selling the motorhome. The sad truth was he had worked his whole career as a travelling salesman, and in 40 years of marriage and raising a family, they had never spent more than a week together by themselves. In just a few weeks on the road, they quickly realized that they couldn't stand spending that much time alone together and ultimately enjoyed doing very different things. Invest time in answering those all important questions now, rather than kicking your bucket list down the road. While I can't guarantee you'll love the answer, I can guarantee that it'll be a much more bitter pill to swallow 10, 20, or 30 years from now if you don't.

Finally, there should be one most obvious reason why you should focus first on those experiences, events, and goals that are at the top of your list or the most difficult to do. If you really want to live a life you love, you don't want to get to the end of it with regrets—regrets about what you didn't do or didn't attempt to do. You can avoid this by making sure you focus on those big-ticket items first, even if it leaves you scrambling to come up with all new goals, new big-ticket items, and new ways in which to invest your time. And that is the best use of that available time, because the things that are most important to you are ultimately the ones that you will most regret not having done when it comes time to walk down the ol' 18th fairway of life. So start today, and once you have had some time to put it together, I'd love to hear about what's on your list at mdowd@oakdalegcc.org.

TAKE A WALK

"All truly great thoughts are conceived by walking."
– Friedrich Nietzsche

We all experience times in our lives when we are stuck. Stuck in a certain place, short of a particular accomplishment, or in particular situations that we need to move past in order to experience personal growth. As golfers, this typically manifests itself at those times in which our games are mired in a slump or when we're having trouble getting past a certain number (like breaking 80 or 100). We seem to be hitting the same bad shots, getting into trouble in the same places, or just unable to play consistently to a level that we know we are capable of. Our games are stuck in a rut, and the longer we are in it, the more it mentally begins to take on a life of its own and the more we need to step away, make a change, and find a way to look at everything from a different perspective and gain a new sense of appreciation for what we're doing. One of the best ways to do this is to take a walk. Literally.

The majority of golf played in the U.S. these days is done so from golf carts, and as a result, a great many of us have almost forgotten what it is even like to walk a round of golf. The advent of the golf cart years ago and the desire for a faster round of golf was not only the death knell for caddies, but seemingly for the experience of walking the golf course in general. And today's fast-paced lifestyle is only adding fuel to the fire and the misconception that riding in carts speeds up a round of golf, when the reality in many cases is just the opposite. Walking the course can sometimes improve the pace of play and very often improves your sense of the pace, but it can also provide a host of other benefits, including physical, social, and even spiritual, that collectively will likely improve not only your score, but your perspective on the experience as a whole.

This overwhelming preference for riding in golf carts when playing isn't the case everywhere, however. A few years ago, I spent some time in England and Scotland playing a few rounds on courses where it is still far more common to walk than ride in "buggies," as they call them, and walking to a degree says as much about how they value the experience as it does their physical conditioning. When it comes to the physical side, there now exists more than enough evidence not only to justify it, but to recommend it. Golfers who walk nine holes will burn an average of 721 calories, while their buggy-bound counterparts weigh in at a mere 411. Walking strengthens the heart, helps the lungs work more efficiently, boosts both the immune and nervous systems, and even helps cognitive function. One study from a Swedish medical university done in 2008 with a sample size of over 300,000 golfers even found the life expectancy of walking golfers to be five years longer than their cart-riding counterparts, more than enough reason alone to engage in the exercise. Now I'm definitely not trying to bad-mouth golf carts, as they do allow untold millions to enjoy this great game (including quite a few at my own club) who would physically be unable to do so otherwise, but at least consider for a moment the fact that if we all walked the course a little more often, we likely wouldn't be cart-bound quite so early in our careers.

If you've spent any time walking a course recently, it's fairly easy to argue its social advantages as well. Sure, when the course is busy, golf carts can provide a lot more downtime, due to the hurry-up-and-wait phenomenon they have inadvertently spawned, but that time is spent with but one of your playing partners at best and completely changes the dynamic and the number of opportunities you have to engage with all your playing partners. And when the course isn't busy? You race from place to place, sometimes even in separate golf carts, instead of conversing and interacting with your partners in a way that brings the entire group together—not unlike that coveted time you all spend at the end of the round in the 19th hole. I remember details of the courses that I walked in England a few years ago and some of the conversations I had then in far greater detail than many of the ones I have played much more recently while riding.

On the spiritual side, I have heard it said before that a walk around the course refreshes the spirit and is as good for the soul as a day spent in church, which is hopefully at least some comfort to those of us who've skipped more than one Sunday service for the lure of the links. It offers a much-needed break from today's modern fast-paced and stress-filled lifestyles as you slow down, breath deeper, and maybe just maybe relax a bit while looking at a familiar course with fresh eyes. It brings your mind, body, and spirit into balance, enlivens your senses, making colors more vibrant and the sounds and smells more alive. You smell the fresh-cut grass, hear the birds more clearly, the rustle of the leaves on the trees, and the crunch of the fallen ones under foot. The babble of the brook (and that of your playing partners) and even that little voice in your head sound a bit different while walking, often allowing you to think more clearly. And at the risk of going to the *Golf in the Kingdom* well one too many times, it reminds me of a passage from that great book where the Scottish Golf Pro Shivas Irons claims, "The gemme was meant for walkin'," upon describing a former member of his club that it was said for whom the walkin' sometimes got so good he forgot to even hit his shots.

In the end, however, I just want you to play golf in whatever way allows you to enjoy the experience most. But if you haven't walked a course lately and need to make a change, haven't figured a way out of that rut, or are just looking for a new experience altogether, then it might just be time to *take a walk*. For as Shivas ultimately said, "If ye can enjoy the walkin', ye can probably enjoy the other times in life when ye're in between. And that's most o' the time' wouldn't ye say?"

JUST ANOTHER DAY IN PARADISE

"Cultivate the habit of being grateful for every good thing that comes to you, and give thanks continuously. And because all things have contributed to your advancement you should include all things in your gratitude."
– Ralph Waldo Emerson

There is an old saying in the golf world that claims that the worst day on the golf course is better than the best day in the office. Well, when your office is the golf course, the lines can start to get a little bit blurred, but let me just start by saying that I count myself as truly blessed to have it that way. Sure, the hours are long, and I work most weekends and holidays, but I get to work each day in a beautiful setting where people convene to relax, enjoy themselves, and recreate. And I help to facilitate all that, and it is something that I enjoy and am grateful to do. It is an infinitesimally small amount of people who are blessed to do what I do, but it is not just that for which I count myself so lucky. Because of this great game and the people who play it, I have a great many other things to be thankful for (family, friends, a home, etc.), and since we're nearing the end of this journey, I thought it might be time to stop and really count our blessings. So here are a few things for you to consider.

If you could fit the entire population of the world into a village consisting of 100 people, maintaining the proportions of all the people living on earth, that village would consist of 60 Asians, 15 Africans, 11 Europeans, and 14 Americans (North, Central and South). There would be 50 women and 50 men. 30 Caucasians and 70 non-Caucasians. There would be 33 Christians, 22 Muslims, 14 Hindu, 7 Buddhists, and 24 who either believe in other minor religions or don't align themselves with any particular faith. Six people would possess almost 60 percent of the wealth, and they would all come from the USA. Almost 50 would live on less than $2 per day. 17 would be illiterate, and only 7 would have a university degree. One person would be dying, one would be being born, and one out of two children would suffer from starvation or malnutrition.

If you woke up this morning in good health, you have more luck than the 1 million people who won't live through the week. If you have never experienced the horror of war, the solitude of prison, the pain of torture, or are not close to death from starvation, then you are better off than 500 million people. If you can go to your place of worship without fear that someone will assault or kill you, then you are luckier than 3 billion people. If you have a full fridge, clothes on your back, a roof over your head, and a place to sleep, you are wealthier than 75 percent of the world's population. If your parents are still alive and still married, you're a rare individual, and if you are reading this message, you're extremely lucky, because you don't comprise the 1.2 billion people who can't read.

These are all fairly sobering statistics and reason enough for me at least to vow to stop complaining about little things like a missed golf shot. But since we're back on the subject of golf, I've got one last statistic for you. If you play golf, you might want to consider yourself among the rarest and luckiest of all individuals, because only one half of one percent of the world's population are fortunate enough to be able to play this great game. So that is why, when people ask me how things are going, I have taken to saying, *"Just another day in paradise."* Not only because it feels good (and really helps you get over those missed shots), but because, you know, it just really is.

AN ODE TO OLD COURSES

"Gratitude bestows reverence, allowing us to encounter everyday epiphanies, those transcendent moments of awe that change forever how we experience life and the world."
– John Milton

Ghosts are not often a subject one associates with the game of golf, but every now and then I am fortunate enough to pass a certain venerable old public course that for some reason causes me to pause and reflect. It is neither historic nor significant, at least not in any of the usual ways, except certainly to the hundreds of thousands of men, women, and children who first learned the game there, played regularly there, or who had their first birdie, eagle, hole-in-one, or under-par round there.

Just as certainly, there are those for whom that old course holds memories of a different sort. For them it serves as a haunting reminder of ignoble acts of frustration: broken clubs, fists shaken at the heavens, and the innumerable expletives and thrown clubs that inevitably follow a case of the shanks or the lost bets that were greater than the bettor could reasonably afford.

The weather-worn old clubhouse still stands perched high upon the bank of a slow-running stream, shabby and outdated, with black-and-white photos of past champions lining the walls, reeking of the memories of past revelry, victories celebrated, and sorrows drowned all at once. A rickety wooden bridge, one originally designed to support walkers and pull carts rather than golf carts, brings you home, spanning the stream that fronts the clubhouse and final green, where the conclusion of each round is played within view of the watchful eyes of the peanut gallery in the clubhouse bar above.

It is just an old course, like many others, but to me it is so much more. It is a place awash with the memories of the trials and triumphs of rounds gone by and the people who played them. Real golf. Real life. Beautifully unadorned, imperfect, and simple, replete with the ghosts of golfers past who remind us simultaneously of our roots, of all that is great and trying about the game, and how thankful we should be that it brings us together with friends to celebrate feats both ordinary and heroic. These ghosts tell the stories of everyday life, one foursome at a time.

Maybe it is because I've grown up playing the game and spent (or misspent) most of my youth and adult life around it and the people and places where it is played, but there are relatively few places in this world that cause me to reflect similarly as do old golf courses. I can recall almost identical feelings upon visiting historic cathedrals and old cemeteries in Europe. Places where time seems to have stood still and where the ghosts of centuries past paint pictures of history in the mind that are nearly as vivid as those depicted so cunningly in the stained glass windows that adorn those cathedral walls. Even so, for me nothing quite rivals old golf courses for evoking this strong sense of emotion, for stirring up memories, and for feeling a sense of connection to the past. There is a certain spirituality and mysticism that surrounds them which at times seems strangely absent to me in many more classically holy places.

And I know I'm not alone. Each year millions of golfers make pilgrimages to the Kingdom of Fife in Scotland, to walk the hallowed grounds of places like Crail, Carnoustie, and The Old Course at St. Andrews, not unlike the millions of Christians who reverently visit Lourdes or the Vatican each year, all while feeling drawn by something akin to the sense of obligation and spiritual completion experienced by the countless Muslims who annually descend upon Mecca. They come seeking the ghosts, as familiar with the game's patron saints—men like Old Tom Morris and Harry Vardon, their stories, and their golfing exploits—as a devout Hindu who has memorized all 700 verses of the

Bhaghavad Gita. They are coming home, to the home of golf that is, armed with their tattered copies of Michael Murphy's *Golf in the Kingdom* or Ben Hogan's *Five Lessons*, rereading and quoting them in the way more religious men might quote a favorite verse from the Bible or the Quran. For them golf is more than just a game—golf is life, not merely a metaphor for it. And it is upon visiting these places that I am at least somewhat inclined to agree.

Fortunately for us devotees to the game in the U.S., there is at least one other place on this earth that inspires a similar sense of reverence and connection to the spirit of the game but which is thankfully a bit closer to home. The Monterey Peninsula. For a golfer, it feels comfortingly like coming home when you visit a place where the lives of just about the entire populace are connected to the game. Monterey may have made its early living by the grace of commercial fishing and its military installations, but not unlike St. Andrews (whose early place in history was due to its famed university rather than its golf courses), Monterey has made its life because of golf, and the men and women who have played there and who still annually flock there to play the game. While the collection of links (and ghosts) in the Monterey aren't quite as old or as historic as their brethren in The Kingdom, they are definitely renowned and some dare say rival their Scottish counterparts for sheer rugged beauty.

I remember my first visit like it was yesterday, playing Pebble Beach at the age of fifteen, just a year removed from Tom

Watson's improbable chip-in on No. 17 to beat my boyhood idol
Jack Nicklaus in the '82 U.S. Open, inking his name indelibly not
only in my mind, but in those of golfers around the world. Even
then I was keenly aware of its history and the stories attached to
the place and I felt truly privileged, almost intimidated by the
opportunity to play as if it were something I had not yet proven
myself worthy of. Fortunately, unlike some things that lose their
luster with age, it feels little different to me today. And while I
have never again been fortunate enough to play on those fabled
links, in the years that followed I have managed to cross most of
the other courses in Monterey off my list, and at nearly every stop
it feels largely the same.

Yes, the ghosts of the game are alive and well on the
Peninsula. You can feel them from afar, when you long for a visit,
as if they're beckoning for your return. And upon that predictable
return, you can feel them in the air, like spirits on the mist that
inhabit the damp fog that rolls in to blanket those links almost
daily. And you can hear them beside the fire, at the Inn at
Spanish Bay, while listening to the bagpipes at dusk and
spinning yarns about the day's exploits to a fellow golfer from
Houston, New York, or even The Kingdom of Fife—one with
whom, though you might have just met, you connect with
instantly. These ghosts aren't threatening; they're like familiar
memories, simultaneously reminding us to slow down,
appreciate, and breathe in the present moment, while keeping us
connected to the lessons and stories of a rich past. So the next

time you visit an old golf course, look for the ghosts and listen for what they have to say. You might not be able to understand them at first, but for every true golfer and at every old course, they are forever whispering, and always saying, *welcome home.*

PLAY EACH ROUND LIKE IT'S YOUR LAST

"Live every day as if it were going to be your last;
for one day you're sure to be right."
– Harry "The Breaker" Harbord Morant

If one were to make a list of themes around which the largest volume of famous quotes that have been passed down through ages were based upon, you could likely argue that "live each day like it's your last" would be at the top of that list. Ever since the Roman Poet Horace implored us to "carpe diem" or "seize the day" in 23 B.C., we have been blessed (or cursed) with similar wisdom by some of the most famous names in history. The philosophy Horace advocated, Epicureanism, based upon the teaching of Epicurus and originating sometime around 307 B.C., essentially espoused pleasure as being the greatest good and could be confused with a hedonistic, almost fatalistic point of view. Fortunately, however, the message has since become about living in a way that will ultimately, when the time comes to leave this life, leave us with few if any regrets.

I was reminded of this message a few years ago when a reader wrote to me and related the story of how the very last thing his father said, shortly after suffering a devastating stroke that would ultimately take his life, was, "I wasn't quite ready to quit golfing yet." It really stopped me at the time, bringing into focus how truly significant the game is in many of our lives. I was reminded again of that story, in ways that hit a bit closer to home, upon my own father's passing when, for reasons most obvious, I was confronted with the obvious fact that one day we will all unfortunately play our last round of golf ... EVER.

Now I understand that this may not be something most of us want to think about, and I am certainly not trying to trivialize anyone's passing. I bring it up, though, because I think it honors the feelings of these men and their obvious passion for and deep relationship with the game and because I believe these feelings are mirrored in a great many of us. In truth, the fact that someday we will play our last round of golf is not something most of us dwell on because we assume that day is still a long way off. If, however, we somehow knew that day wasn't so terribly far away, would we do it any differently? Would we spend our time on the course differently, act differently, interact with our playing partners differently, or potentially even play the game in a different way? Henry David Thoreau once said, "You must live in the present, launch yourself on every wave, find your eternity in each moment. Fools stand on their island of opportunities and look toward another land. There is no other land; there is no other life but this." And there may be no other game than this— the one we play today.

Ultimately, however, and at the risk of sounding a bit like a broken record at this point, we should all by now understand that golf is so much more than just a game. For most of us, it is a way of life, a way in which we come together with friends and family to socialize and recreate, to live, laugh, love, honor, respect, and support those we are most close to. And for some fortunate ones of us, it is simultaneously how we make our living.

Speaking for myself, golf has pretty much been my life since about the age of seven. It is how I chose to make my living. And while the time demands of making that living, combined with family and having young children, has to a degree forced my own golf game a bit to the back-burner in the past handful of years, the inability to play as much as I would like has made me value those opportunities I do have to get out there even more. I try to talk to my partners more, enjoy the beauty of the course more, spend less time in my own head worrying about my game, and just appreciate being blessed to spend that time with friends and family in such an idyllic environment. I take my students or my daughters out to the course more and sometimes don't even bring my clubs, choosing instead to focus on helping them to learn the lessons and things that I think will help them enjoy the game more and get more out of it. Don't get me wrong—I still endeavor to play well, and one day when and *IF* I have more time and if possibly one of my girls takes up the game in earnest, I will hopefully have the opportunity to invest the amount of time it takes to play the game at or above the level I did in my younger days. But that is a very big *if*.

Time is the part of that last statement itself that predictably leads us back to my original thought. We all generally assume we have more time—more time to do the things we haven't done, more time to live the life we want to live, more time to love those we most love, and for us golfers, more time for another round, another day. Someday, however, we will all play our last round of golf and most of us won't even know that it will have been our last round when it takes place... Albert Camus once said, "Don't wait for the last judgment, for it comes every day." And so as if in anticipation of that judgment, let us make sure that every day we live in accordance with our ideals, and let us not put off what we know we *would* do if we actually knew we were lacing up those spikes for the last time, leaving us to look back with regret for not having made it everything it could and should be. And with that ultimate thought in mind, I suggest you consider these few questions.

If we were to assume that our next round would be our last round, wouldn't we be a better playing partner—or fellow competitor for that matter—winning with class or losing with grace? Wouldn't we be a better person to be around and conduct ourselves in a way that we would if we thought our five-year-old child or grandchild was watching? Wouldn't we really take a look around, each and every hole, and appreciate the true beauty that surrounds us, rather than focusing upon the one or two small areas that are slightly less than perfect? And speaking of our beautiful surroundings, wouldn't we always take care of the course and the club in a way that left it better than we found it? Wouldn't we show the sort of oft-mentioned integrity real golfers lay claim to and finally play the ball as it lies, try our best on every shot, post that final score (accurately), and even if only once, call a penalty on ourselves when no one else was watching? And lastly, but definitely not least, wouldn't we play the game with a level of love, gratitude, and appreciation for it that honors all those who have gone before us, those who have made it possible for us to play, and those for whom playing the game is no longer a possibility? I think so, because if golf really is more important and more sacred than just a game, if golf truly is life, shouldn't you *play each round like it's your last*? I believe you should, because you know what? If you do, one day you're sure to be right.

> *"Alas for those that never sing,*
> *and die with all their music left in them."*
> – Oliver Wendell Holmes

CARPE DIEM!

ABOUT THE AUTHOR

"This is the true joy in life, the being used for a purpose recognized by yourself as a mighty one; the being a force of nature instead of a feverish, selfish little clod of ailments and grievances complaining that the world will not devote itself to making you happy. I am the opinion that my life belongs to the whole community, and as long as I live it is my privilege to do for it whatever I can. I want to be thoroughly used up when I die, for the harder I work the more I live. I rejoice in life for its own sake. Life is no "brief candle" for me. It is a sort of splendid torch which I have got hold of for the moment, and I want to make it burn as brightly as possible before handing it on to future generations."
– George Bernard Shaw

Mike Dowd has been the Head PGA Professional at Oakdale Golf & Country Club in Oakdale, California since 2001. He is currently serving his third term on the Northern California PGA Board of Directors and is the Chairman of their Committee for the Growth of the Game. He has introduced thousands of people to the game of golf since turning professional in 1990 and has coached players that have played golf collegiately at the University of Hawaii, San Francisco, U.C. Berkeley, U.C. Davis, University of the Pacific, C.S.U. Sacramento, C.S.U. Stanislaus, C.S.U. Chico, and Missouri Valley State, as well as on both men's and ladies' professional tours.

Mike currently lives in Turlock, California with his wife Julieanne and their two aspiring LPGA stars, Isabella (age 9) and Nicoletta (age 6). In Turlock he is the Chairman of the City of Turlock's Parks & Recreation Commission, serves on the Turlock Community Theatre Board of Directors, and is a member of the Kiwanis Club of Greater Turlock. In his spare time (what's that?) he enjoys playing golf with his girls, music, fishing, and following the foibles of the Sacramento Kings, the San Francisco 49ers, the San Francisco Giants, and, of course, the PGA Tour. You can find him at mikedowdgolf.com

Made in the USA
Middletown, DE
15 February 2016